TELEVISION ADVERTISING THAT WORKS

TELEVISION ADVERTISING THAT WORKS

An Analysis of Commercials From Effective Campaigns

Stephen W. Marshall
and
Marilyn S. Roberts

CAMBRIA
PRESS

AMHERST, NEW YORK

Requests for permission should be directed to:
permissions@cambriapress.com, or mailed to:
Cambria Press
20 Northpointe Parkway, Suite 188
Amherst, NY 14228

Library of Congress Cataloging-in-Publication Data

Marshall, Stephen W.
   Television advertising that works : an analysis of commercials from effective campaigns / Stephen W. Marshall, Marilyn S. Roberts.
        p. cm.
   Includes bibliographical references and index.
   ISBN 978-1-60497-513-0 (alk. paper)
   1. Television advertising—Research. 2. Advertising—Research.
I. Roberts, Marilyn Sue, 1949- II. Title.

   HF6146.T42M37 2008
   659.1'43—dc22

2008012210

I dedicate this work to my family. God is love.
—Stephen W. Marshall

To Jerry, for his love and encouragement
to always follow my dreams,
and to Michael and Justin,
truly my greatest blessings on earth
—Marilyn S. Roberts

TABLE OF CONTENTS

LIST OF FIGURE AND TABLES

EXECUTIVE SUMMARY

The research contained in this book contributes to the theoretical and practical knowledge of message strategies and the executional devices used in U.S. television advertising. Using rigorous content analysis, the authors investigated characteristics of commercials from among EFFIE Award winners of 1999 through 2004—advertising originating from "effective" campaigns. This work contributes to advertising research by examining the predictive congruency of the FCB advertising planning grid with message strategies found in EFFIE commercials; overall EFFIE commercial message strategy (based on Laskey, Day, & Crask, 1989) and tactic relationships (based on Stewart & Furse, 1986); and content analysis methodology relative to improving objectivity and assessing reliability.

This work examines the FCB grid (Vaughn, 1980), used in many advertising courses as a means to approach advertising planning. It looks at congruency of message strategy (informational or transformational) as measured by Laskey et al. (1989). Results discussed here offer minimum predictive support in terms of the product categories on the FCB grid used to originate message strategy.

Message strategy findings indicate EFFIE commercials exhibit characteristics that contribute positively to dependent evaluations of advertising effectiveness as measured by Stewart and Furse (1986). Examples of these characteristics include:

- Humorous tone
- Memorable rhymes
- Presence of music
- Slogans and mnemonic devices
- Visual memory devices

However, many differences exist, specifically with the presence (or absence) of brand-differentiating messages in EFFIE advertising.

Overall, EFFIE commercials tend toward the emotional (48%) or a balance of rational and emotional (43%), compared to rational (8%) alone. EFFIE commercials show a trend toward more transformational (emotional) message strategies over time, specifically in terms of strategies focusing on user and brand image, with use occasion on the increase by year as well. In addition, most product categories exhibited transformational strategies over time with no specific product category having a relationship with informational strategies alone.

This research examines the dominant characteristics found in informational and transformational message strategies exhibited by EFFIE commercials. Informational commercials exhibited relationships with the following:

- Balance of rational and emotional appeals
- Brand-differentiating message

- Indirect comparisons
- Memorable rhymes
- Presenter or spokesperson on camera
- Product performance as main benefit
- Slogans or mnemonic devices
- Substantive supers (words on the screen reinforcing a product characteristic or as part of the commercial message)

Commercials exhibiting a transformational strategy used tactics such as:

- Appeals focusing on excitement
- Enjoyment appeals
- Formats creating a mood or image
- Music as a major element
- Presence of a background cast
- Presence of male main characters
- Presence of racial or ethnic minority characters in minor roles
- Product reminder as main message
- Racial or ethnic minorities as main characters
- Sensation or variety

Lastly, this research provides a thorough review of content analysis methodology, argues for the need to improve reliability of measure when conducting content analyses, and offers suggestions for improving objectivity and intercoder reliability assessment.

PREFACE

Twenty years have passed since Stewart and Furse (1986) published their landmark study, *Effective Television Advertising: A Study of 1,000 Commercials*. Their groundbreaking study serves as the benchmark for many follow-up studies evaluating television advertising effectiveness and commercial content elements. We have based our book on that study, and we wish to thank those authors for their rich contribution to the literature. We hope this study complements theirs and contributes to future researchers' evaluations of message strategies and tactical elements in commercials.

Advertising effectiveness—an elusive phrase—resists a single definition. It means many things to many people in different situations. We intend here to look at message strategies that work in effective campaign commercials and not to define advertising effectiveness. The EFFIE awards, sponsored by the American

Marketing Association (AMA), provide a framework of commercials to investigate, and we appreciate the AMA's cooperation.

This study focuses on producing a benchmark for comparison studies examining differences in message strategies across cultures. The research herein provides a methodological framework for producing comparative studies examining television commercials and other video content (i.e., delivered over the Internet) across cultures.

The authors owe much to the wonderful support of faculty and staff at the University of Florida. John C. Sutherland, Richard J. Lutz, and Debbie M. Treise all contributed to this work, and we thank them for their support. In addition, the University of Florida's Advertising Department and its students provided valuable assistance. This research required a team of coders who worked very hard to produce the best work possible. The authors wish to acknowledge their effort and to thank them.

TELEVISION ADVERTISING
THAT WORKS

CHAPTER 1

INTRODUCTION

We find that advertising works the way the grass grows. You can never see it, but every week you have to mow the lawn.

—Andy Tarshis, A. C. Nielsen

The business of the U.S. media accounts for 5% of the country's gross domestic product, reaches hundreds of millions of consumers daily, and has tremendous global influence (Schasky, 2006). Within this media framework, individual companies spend millions on what they hope will be effective advertising for their organizations. However, evaluating the true dimensions of effective advertising has proven difficult (Frandin, Sheehan, & Patti, 1992; Moriarty, 1996). Academic literature defines models of advertising effects but tends to measure it by various individual dimensions of effectiveness. Likewise, effectiveness measures often depend on the goals of a communication campaign and differ across campaigns (Frandin et al., 1992; Moriarty, 1996). As marketers struggle to have their voices heard in a changing and dynamic media landscape, gaining knowledge of advertising effectiveness becomes more significant.

Television advertising combines sight and sound—one of only a few forms of marketing communication with the ability to do so. However, television advertising is experiencing a sea change. Some industry professionals proclaim that television advertising has begun to die a slow death, while other professionals simply consider the industry ill. For example, in 2005, Unilever reported slashing its television advertising budget by 20% over its previous three annual budgets in favor of relationship-driven Internet executions or outdoor advertising (Terazono, 2005). Furthermore, in 2005, for the first time in 30 years, Heineken moved its dollars completely from television advertising budgets into sponsorship and point-of-sales promotions because they lacked confidence in television advertising (Walsh, 2005). These represent just two examples of how brand managers and agencies search for ways to use new technology for advertising delivery (Maddox, 2006).

Still, even with some marketing emphasis moving away from television, the medium continues to provide an outlet of reach and frequency to an unmatched degree. Likewise, much of what we would consider traditional television advertising—commercial messages—has moved to the Internet. Advertising expenditures for the Internet increased from $600 million in 1996 to over $9 billion as of 2006 (DMA, 2007). Many advertisers are wondering how to revamp traditional television content for the Internet. The advertiser's need to understand the components of effective television advertising increases with the rise of technology, and these opportunities give video content providers new avenues for reaching consumers.

PURPOSE AND SIGNIFICANCE OF STUDY

In this book, we provide a comprehensive and thorough investigation of message strategies and devices found in television advertisements from U.S. industry-judged-effective (EFFIE) advertising campaigns. Rather than measure the many dependent contributors to advertising effectiveness, this book will focus on the commercial itself. In this sense, this research differs from others; we examine actual commercials from campaigns deemed effective by industry peers. In other words, rather than look at single item measures typically used to evaluate advertising, this study examines the actual effectiveness winners.

We selected the EFFIE awards as a sample frame of advertisements since these commercials come from effective campaigns. Frazer, Sheehan, and Patti (2002) suggested the AMA's EFFIE awards as a valuable data set for understanding the relationship between advertising strategy and advertising effectiveness. Frazer et al. (2002) commented:

> While it certainly cannot be said whether the commercials in the sample used in this study were judged as being effective based on cognitive effects or on behavioural outcomes, it is known that they were judged as being effective based on concrete evidence of one or the other. Thus, effective advertising is operationalized as the receipt of an industry effectiveness award. (p. 152)

In addition, Wright et al. (1997) considered the EFFIEs a potential source of useful data since competitors must provide the problem background, objectives, creative and media strategy, and evidence of results. Moreover, a descriptive study of this type would be less telling if a strong theory of advertising effectiveness existed (Stewart & Furse, 1986).

OUTLINE

In chapter 2, we review the relevant literature regarding the current state of the television industry, advertising effectiveness, and proposed models of how effectiveness occurs. This discussion includes hierarchy-of-effect models such as the Elaboration Likelihood Model, the FCB grid, the Rossiter-Percy grid, and Taylor's Strategy Wheel. It also includes literature relating to message typologies and execution tactics and establishes the framework for measuring the characteristics of the television advertising investigated herein.

In chapter 3, we detail the unit of analysis and content analysis approach used to investigate EFFIE commercials, making an effort to raise the quality of the content analysis above the typically acceptable standards. In chapter 4, we review the results of the study, and in chapter 5, we conclude, discuss research limitations, and explore future research possibilities.

CHAPTER 2

BACKGROUND

Television combines sight and sound to give the media consumer and advertiser benefits unavailable from any other media. Television has the ability to be true to life and pervasive (Katz, 2003). According to a study conducted by Veronis, Suhler, and Stevensen (2002) the average person will spend 1,745 hours a year with television. Compare this to 1,002 hours with radio, 184 hours with recorded music, 171 hours with newspapers, 176 hours with the Internet, and 121 hours with magazines. Daily time with television has also increased over the last decade. In 1970, the average household viewed close to six hours a day while in 2004 the average household viewed over eight hours (Nielsen Media Research [NMR], 2004). The reach of television far exceeds other media with 90% of adults 18+ viewing some television per day compared to radio at 73% reach, newspapers at 65%, the Internet at 51% reach, and magazines reaching 48%

of adults per day (NMR, 2003). Television is central to the lives and culture of America.

TELEVISION ADVERTISING

Most advertising in television typically involves embedding the advertising within television programming content. Commercials can be delivered in numerous ways: participation in or a national buy gives the advertiser national reach, while a spot announcement delivered via the local cable or affiliate station and syndicated programs provides advertisers unique coverage opportunities (Wells, Moriarty & Burnett, 2006). Though once a pillar for national reach and mass audiences, broadcast networks lose audience share every year. By 2005, the average share of audience for cable television, 51.8, dwarfed the share for the combined seven traditional broadcast networks—45.9 (Lafayette, 2005). As a result, much of the television advertising money traditionally going to mass-audience-affiliated broadcast networks now appears to flow into more target-specific cable networks. Broadcast networks such as NBC have seen their early 2005 performance numbers for prime time decline, with some programs losing as much as 15% of their audience compared to last year. Furthermore, the 2005 upfront sales market for NBC plummeted to $800 million from the previous year's $2 billion. Overall, broadcast network advertising expenditures have dropped from $11.9 billion to $11.2 billion in the years 2004 to 2005. The trend continues with advertisers leaving network television because prices continue to increase as audiences continue to decrease. In fact, not only are advertising inventories going unsold compared to years past, but also the loss of audience is creating an environment of what advertisers call *makegoods* (Lafayette, 2005). Makegoods compensate advertisers for spots that miss audience delivery contractual agreements or for missed airings (Arens, 2004). Fragmentation and increasing clutter contribute to the movement away from placing advertising with traditional mass audience broadcast networks.

Fragmentation and Clutter

Technology has created an ever-selective and mobile audience empowering the media consumer with choice. At the same time, this evolving and growing media landscape has given marketers new and exciting opportunities to promote their brand. However, media growth has produced media fragmentation. Because of this technology growth, we have seen the consumer's average daily exposures to marketing communication balloon from 500 to 2,000 messages in the 1970s upwards to 5,000 messages a day in 2005 (Howard, 2005). In this fragmented landscape we need not wonder why evaluating advertising effectiveness matters to marketers.

Generally, fragmentation is as much a cause as it is an effect. Jupiter Research analyst David Schatsky (2006) considered *fragmentation* dynamic and occurring simultaneously in three dimensions: audience fragmentation, personal fragmentation, and media fragmentation. Each form of fragmentation feeds off the other, and as technology continues to change traditional advertising models, marketers must remain fluid and adaptive.

The erosion of the traditional mass media audience, or *audience fragmentation*, occurs because of increasing media and entertainment choices. *Personal fragmentation* becomes a product of audience fragmentation since consumers spread their time across new media (Schatsky, 2006). Table 1 shows some examples of audience fragmentation from a study conducted by Fielding and Bahary (2005) for Starcom. For example, comparing the media industry from the 1980s until 2004 shows the number of commercial TV stations has gone up 92%, the average number of cable channels has increased 836%, cable penetration has increased 130%, and home-computer penetration has increased 1,220%. All of these new alternatives fragment audiences for media content providers. Audience fragmentation is not confined solely to traditional media but also comes from the Internet, where younger audiences spend more of their time (Feldstein, 2005). *Ad Age*'s 2006 Fact Pack reported a study conducted by eMarketer concluding that out of 283.4 million people in the U.S. ages 3+: 38.1% were not online yet, 24.8% were dialup Internet users, and 37.1% were broadband users. The same study predicts the number of nonusers and dialup users will convert to broadband use and will contribute to increasing broadband penetration an additional 11% by the year 2008. Broadband penetration is important to note due to its capacity to deliver video content.

Even with the growth of traditional and alternative media choices, television has hope in this audience-fragmented marketplace because of one element: content loyalty. Research

TABLE 1. Media time comparison.

	1980s	2004/2005
Number of Commercial TV Stations	700	1,345
Average Number of TV Sets per Home	1.8	2.6
Average Number of Channels Available per TV Household	11	103
Three-Network Prime-Time Household Share	75%	36%
Cable Penetration (+ADS)	40%	92%
VCR Penetration	1%	87%
Remote-Control Penetration	50%	95%
Number of Radio Stations	8,748	13,838
Home-Computer Penetration	5%	66%
Number of Consumer Magazines	1,500	5,340

conducted by eMarketer found the average television viewer spends 34.5 hours per week watching television while viewing the same 13.6 channels. The study found consistent results with other media as well. Internet users spent an average of 7.5 hours per week surfing the Web but limited their surfing time to an average of 17 sites. The average radio listener spent her/his weekly time with an average of only 3.2 stations (Mandeses, 2005). In addition, a study conducted by Nielsen Media Research (2003) reports that even consumers with the option to view up to 120 channels on average still only view 16.5 channels. Those who can view 120 channels average one additional channel compared to the average of those who can view only 51–60 channels. Loyalty remains a constant regardless of the medium and amount of choices.

In addition to audience and personal fragmentation, *media fragmentation* has also occurred. Media fragmentation refers to the individualizing of content in any form such as broadcasters and/or cable companies offering á la carte content, individual songs, personalized reading lists, or any other situation with individualized, delivered content (Schatsky, 2006). In terms of television, media fragmentation involves the selective personalization of programming as well as the ability for á la carte delivery of video content to alternative viewing devices.

The selective personalization of content on the television screen comes from the increasing aid of digital video recorders (DVRs) and video-on-demand (VOD) options. To sum it up best, digital video recorders are to digital television what VCRs were to analog, while video-on-demand allows viewers to choose from stored content. Both allow a viewer to use a digital guide provided by the cable/satellite company or a third party to select television content. DVRs and VOD also enable the viewer to pause, rewind, and fast forward recorded programming. Viewers can typically procure DVR service through digital cable and satellite providers; however, third-party companies such as TiVo Inc. produce a stand-alone DVR and service package. TiVo is intuitive compared to the typical DVR because the service cross-tabulates the programming the viewer likes and records similar programs for later viewing.

Both TiVos and standard DVRs challenge advertising effectiveness given their increasing popularity. In March 2006, Interpublic media-buying giant Magna Global USA reported DVR penetration in the U.S. at 11.7%—up 10% from the previous quarter. Current projections indicate DVR penetration should reach 34.4 million by 2010 (Mandese, 2006). An online study conducted by Mindshare found 88% of respondents who currently own a DVR bought it to watch programs at their convenience, and 77% purchased a DVR because it allows them to skip commercials (Consoli, 2005). Consumer choice in selecting content as well as their ability to skip commercials concerns advertisers.

VOD continues to gain popularity as well. Magna Global USA expects that 66 million households will have access to programming delivered via VOD by 2010, compared to 24.5 million households measured in the first quarter of 2005 (Mandese, 2006). VOD has yet to realize a consistent revenue model and VOD content providers continue to test market different plans. Some content providers charge á la carte for programs with and without advertising, while others embed commercials and deliver content for free. For example, in a recent agreement between CBS and Comcast, the broadcaster plans to release episodes of *CSI, NCIS, Survivor,* and *Amazing Race* 24 hours after their prime-time airing. CBS plans on keeping the original commercials in each broadcast and will charge $0.99 per episode (www.cbs.com). Although others have followed this model, a recent Adage.com survey found 65% of voters said they would not pay for on-demand content that contains commercials (Klaassen, 2005). Overall, it is still too early to determine a specific VOD-pricing model. Moreover, even with the increased penetration of DVRs and VOD technology, it does not appear this technology changes the amount of time we consume television, only the way we consume it. The individual viewing time remains constant between owners and nonowners of this technology: an average of 3.9 hours daily (Myers, 2004).

In addition to DVRs and VOD allowing consumers to personalize what they view on their television screen, consumers can choose to view traditional television content on alternative devices. Much of the delivery of this content is still in test, but in 2006 *Television Week* projected $270 million in upfront commitments going to cross-platform, on-demand offerings from networks. Although only 3% of the total $9 billion projected, it still represents a significant change and a new means for advertisers to expand their reach using traditional television advertising (Spotsndots, 2006).

Many players already participate in the mobile video-delivery game, including Apple's iTunes, America Online, Google's Google Video and Yahoo!, in addition to program availability directly from the broadcasters' Web sites (Caplan, 2006). Viewers can play downloadable video content on any mobile device able to play digital video such as an Apple iPod or a video-enabled cellular phone. Viewing has moved to cell phones as well. eMarketer reports 3% of mobile phone subscribers view television content on their phone, with the number projected to hit 15% by 2009. Web sites are also experimenting with video advertising. Companies such as Intel have moved traditional commercials to Internet sites such as ESPN and Yahoo!, and eMarketer projects online video advertising spending will reach $640 million in 2007 and $1.5 billion by 2009 (Maddox, 2006).

The future remains uncertain and technology clouds the video delivery models. Some see advertising models becoming user specific, basing targeting on opt-in characteristics and by tracking downloads of content. Others see pricing as an issue: viewers who consider it too high opt for current entertainment, thus leading to slower adoption of trends (www.tvn.com, 2006). Fragmentation—audience, personal, and media—contributes to the importance of making television advertising more effective.

Commercial Clutter

Not only are all forms of fragmentation an issue for television advertising effectiveness, but also the increase in commercial clutter has raised cause for concern. The television viewer experiences clutter during commercial breaks when the quantity of messages compete for attention (Azzaro, 2004). Clutter has increased with increasing commercial time per hour over the years. In the 1960s, a time with fewer television networks, commercial breaks totaled 8 minutes per hour (Strachan, 2005). From the 1960s until 2002, that time doubled to 16 minutes an hour during prime time (Arens, 2006). As of 2005, 18 minutes of every prime-time program is reserved for commercial breaks and commercial minutes increase to 21 for daytime programming (Strachan, 2005).

In addition to increasing commercial minutes per program, programmers and advertisers increase clutter within commercial breaks by buying smaller commercial units. For over three decades, the 30-second spot ruled as the standard unit in television advertising, with the 15-second spot a recent popular alternative. Because of fragmentation, advertisers now look for new and even smaller spot availabilities. Recently, advertisers have gone as short as :05 seconds. The :05-second spot, referred to as the *pod puncher* (*pod* refers to the time when commercials air within a program), would run in the same break with a 30-second spot. The strategy behind is to increase spot awareness by using the pod puncher as a cue for the commercial to come later in the same commercial break (McClellan, 2006).

The growth in fragmentation and clutter has diluted the confidence advertisers have in television commercials. Even though traditional television viewing habits have changed, the television commercial remains important for all types of video content. For the advertiser, the growth of nontraditional viewing combined with the integration of advertising within these new avenues has shifted the emphasis from traditional exposure philosophies to more of a mindset of engagement.

Engagement
The term *engagement* became a hot topic in the advertising world in 2005 and continues as a highly contested term. Barbara Bacci-Mirque, senior vice president for the Association of National Advertisers (ANA) reports, "ANA members have told us that—in the face of media fragmentation and consumer control over how they receive advertising messages—new forms of advertising are needed to reach today's consumers. In this age of accountability, new metrics are necessary to adequately reflect the impact of nontraditional messages" (Advertising Research Foundation [ARF], 2005). This perceived need for the new measurement term arose from the need to measure new technology such as blogs and gaming, as well as mobile devices (Pilotta, 2005). No longer do Nielsen Media numbers describe reach and frequency sufficiently to measure impressions leading to advertising effectiveness. Advertisers want return on investment (ROI) or return on objectives (ROO) engagement evidence for

the commercials they run on television and elsewhere (Consoli, 2006).

Interestingly enough, according to the *Merriam-Webster's Dictionary* (1997), engagement has four different meanings: appointment, employment, a mutual promise to marry, and a hostile encounter. Regardless of its definition, in nonmedia terms, the ANA, the American Association of Advertising Agencies, and ARF have embraced it as a possible metric to replace frequency in media planning. Joe Plummer, chief research officer at ARF, defined engagement at the 2006 ARF *re:Think* conference as follows: "Engagement is turning on a prospect to a brand idea enhanced by the surrounding context" (Creamer, 2006). ARF has spearheaded the engagement initiative, which is still under construction.

One attempt at operationalizing television commercial engagement came in the 4th quarter of 2005 from an agreement between *Court TV* and Starcom. The agreement adds a viewer-engagement component, which includes a proprietary viewer-attention component and a viewer-retention component. These proprietary engagement components are then applied to the standard Nielsen Media impression number to achieve an overall engagement factor (Consoli, 2006).

Measuring engagement continues as a work in progress. However the industry decides to measure engagement, a single metric is unlikely since the term can and has been defined in many different ways. The Magazine Publishers of America (MPA) (2006) published an extensive and thorough white paper discussing the development of and aspects contributing to the engagement measure. According to their study and survey of the literature, engagement has many meanings. Terms often associated with engagement include: involvement, connection, resonance, stickiness, experience, wantedness, and relationship. The MPA (2006) discusses three main factors that affect engagement: the message and the quality of the creative; the media environment; and the mindset of the consumer relative to situations of receptivity and physical conditions. In addition to the synonymous terms and the main affecting factors, the MPA (2006) believes engagement should help the marketing communicator understand multitasking media use. As reported by MindShare MORe Panel, of adults 18+ in October 2001 to February 2002, only 7% of respondents reported not multitasking during television viewing. This classified television as the least engaging medium, with radio (23%), newspapers (44%), and magazines (50%) faring better.

The concept of engagement—at least at the message and quality of the creative level—is central to this research. Although current research focuses on television commercials, we can make greater use of these findings in terms of designing video content for other media. New technology gives advertisers ways of delivering traditional commercials outside the realm of the television set. Moreover, technology has given consumers more choices as well as the ability to take control of content decisions. In other words, the use of media is shifting from a passive role to a more active search dynamic. This shift will take advertising content once produced for television to realms of alternative delivery. Although the measures included in this research are confined to examining the television commercial, the peer-reviewed effectiveness context from which the sample is derived should be considered. A further understanding of relationships and associations regarding product categories, executional, and message strategy elements over time allows the advertiser to take what we learn from television commercials and apply those concepts to expanding media opportunities. If we intend to further our understanding of advertising engagement, commercials from peer-reviewed effective campaigns offer a good place to start.

Television Advertising Expenditures
While audience fragmentation challenges television program-mers, advertisers look to engagement or another relevant ways to justify advertising ROI. Even with the change and growing uncertainty, evidence through the continued growth of adver-tising expenditures provides some reassurance that advertising on television remains a viable way to reach a mass audience. However, we see a noted shift occurring from traditional broad-cast network television to cable. This change of dollars from broadcast television to cable television shows up in 2004 U.S. media expenditures. Even with the shift, television broadcast networks still dominate as a place for advertisers to spend their money. According to the *Adage 2005 FactPack*, broadcast tele-vision ranked third behind direct mail and newspapers in over-all advertising expenditures with total expenditures reaching $41.93 billion. This shows a decrease of .3% from 2003. The top seven broadcast networks by advertising revenue were:

- CBS ($5,828 million)
- NBC ($5,576 million)
- ABC ($5,127 million)
- FOX ($3,001 million)
- WB ($1,024 million)
- UPN ($505 million)
- PAX ($162 million)

Although cable ranked fifth in overall advertising expendi-tures behind radio ($19.1 billion) at $18.81 billion, the industry grew 15.4% compared to 2003. The top five cable networks by revenue include:

- ESPN ($1,164 million)
- Nickelodeon ($844 million)
- MTV ($836 million)
- Lifetime ($832 million)
- TBS ($753 million)

All five top cable networks achieved double-digit increases in revenue from 2003 with ESPN capturing the most at 26.4%.

Top Television Advertisers

The *2005 Ad Age Fact Pack* reports companies featuring nondurable goods, automobiles, personal-care/pharmaceuticals, and media products dominate the top five television advertising expenditure positions for network, cable, spot, and syndicated television. Proctor and Gamble (P&G) ranked first in overall expenditures for network television ($833.6 million), cable television ($514.6 million), and syndicated television ($329.2 million). General Motors ranked second to P&G in network television ($641.4 million) and cable television ($311.3 million) expenditures. Automobile companies dominated the spot television market with DaimlerChrysler ($596 million), General Motors ($393 million), Honda Motors ($330.9 million), Nissan Motor ($320.1 million), and Ford Motor Company ($277.8 million) occupying the top five spots. Looking across all television spending categories, other important television advertising spenders include Johnson and Johnson, ranking third in network television spending ($527.5 million) and second in syndicated television ($101.5 million) spending, Pfizer ranking fifth in network television spending ($442.4 million) and fourth in syndicated television spending ($84.9 million), and Altria Group ranking fourth in cable television ($187.4 million). Media giants Time Warner ($250.1 million) and Walt Disney ($168.3 million) came in third and fifth in cable spending, respectively.

ADVERTISING AGENCIES

The advertising industry has also undergone change over the last decade. Consolidation has transformed the advertising agency business, and a few large holding companies now control a majority of the work the overall industry produces. Consolidation allows agencies to serve their clients better by becoming more integrated in promotional and marketing services. Consolidation also allows large agency groups to purchase media time in bulk, producing more revenue. By the mid-1990s, the global share of the top ten agency networks had doubled over 10 years from 22.9% to 48.3%. By 2004, the top four agency groups controlled 55% of all global advertising billings and 82% of all U.S. advertising billings (Mueller, 2004). According to the *2004 Advertising Age Agency Report* by Adage, the top four global marketing organizations by revenue included Omnicom Group ($8,621.4 million), WPP Group ($6,756.1 million), Interpublic Group of Companies ($5,863.4 million), and Publicis Groupe ($4,408.9 million). Each of these marketing groups controls numerous agency brands. According to the *2004 Advertising Age Agency Report* by Adage, the top ten U.S. agency brands by revenue include:

- JWT (WPP, $456.2 million)
- Leo Burnett Worldwide (Publicis, $404.2 million)
- McCann Erickson Worldwide (Interpublic, $300 million)
- BBDO Worldwide (Omnicom, $279.1 million)
- Grey Worldwide (Grey, $270.5 million)

- DDB Worldwide Communications (Omnicom, $252.3 million)
- Ogilvy & Mather Worldwide (WPP, $235.6 million)
- Foote Cone & Belding Worldwide (Interpublic, $221.6 million)
- Y&R (WPP, $215.7 million)
- Publicis Worldwide (Publicis, $200.9 million)

Advertising Awards

Fierce competition takes place among marketing and agency groups. Winning awards is one way agencies can differentiate themselves from other agencies. Advertising awards, an important part of the industry, number over 500 worldwide (Polonsky & Waller, 1996).This includes both national and international awards, including the Cannes, London International Awards, Mobius Advertising Awards, Cresta International Advertising Awards, International Automotive Advertising Awards, Ad-Awards.com International Advertising Awards, Addy Awards, John Caples International Awards, Webby Awards, The Roses Advertising Awards, Clio Awards, and EFFIE Awards. Advertising awards recognize outstanding work, and agencies receive them for a variety of reasons. Some awards cover a wide range of products, media, and services, while others focus on specific elements of advertising within a particular medium or by the overall creative idea (Helgesen, 1994).

By competing and winning awards, advertising agencies gain recognition for their work, encourage creativity among staff members, increase industry prestige, and promote themselves to potential clients (Schweitzer & Hester, 1992). Helgesen (1994) explored the issues of advertising awards by surveying 40 advertising representatives of the 10 largest advertising agencies in Norway. All respondents were employees of

U.S.-owned network agency brands. Results concluded that employees perceived the awards as symbols of creative excellence and professional leadership. Polonsky and Waller (1995) examined the impact of winning advertising awards on billings and revenue for agencies in Australia with results indicating no revenue effect based on the number of awards won. This led the authors to conclude advertising agencies compete for awards primarily for nonmonetary reasons.

While some advertising agencies will argue for the significance of creative awards, others will argue that effectiveness awards are paramount. During her keynote address at the 2005 EFFIE awards ceremony, Cheryl Bermen, Leo Burnett USA chairman and chief creative officer, opined that industry focuses too much on abstract creativity and not enough on effective results (Creamer & Arndorfer, 2005).

EFFIE Awards
The AMA started the EFFIE Awards in 1968, and the advertising industry recognizes it as the only national award that honors achievement in meeting and exceeding advertising goals and objectives. Top marketing and advertising management, research, and creative executives in the advertising industry serve as judges for the award. Awards go each year to the top advertising producers in each product category with one overall grand EFFIE winner chosen. Robert Scarpelli, chairman and chief creative officer of U.S. DDB Chicago, stated, "Our reason for being is to provide better ideas that lead to better results for our clients. I believe that they aren't better ideas if they don't deliver better results. And that you can't get better results if you don't have better ideas. The EFFIEs are the only awards that corroborate that our ideas lead to results. They prove we're not doing this to make our reels better."

In the first of two phases, EFFIE judges evaluate case briefs submitted by agencies on a stand-alone basis, without comparison to other entries within a particular product category and without creative materials. In the second phase, judges review finalists within the same product category based on case brief and creative scores. The final score derives from the average of the brief score and the creative score with the brief score weighted 2:1 to emphasize effectiveness. The brief must contain all evidence of results, and the AMA has the right to verify any claims or the entry risks disqualification.

The EFFIE awards are not without critics. Moriarty (1996) examined the objectives and evaluation mechanisms used to evaluate advertising effectiveness in EFFIE campaign submissions. In her content analysis of 29 EFFIE entries, she found 17% stated measurable objectives, 50% represented communication objectives, 25% delineated marketing effect (sales or share) objectives and 25% included a mix of both. Results showed 91% of the campaigns clearly linked to objectives, but fewer than 10% made causal arguments linking the affect stated in the objective to the advertising message.

ADVERTISING EFFECTIVENESS

We can evaluate advertising effectiveness in a number of ways, and, importantly, we must delineate the terms *effects* and *effectiveness* since the current study concerns itself specifically with effectiveness, which differs from effects. Isolating advertising effectiveness proves difficult, given the complexity of the marketing environment, while the many parts of the marketing process collectively affect the success of a product or service (Wright-Isak, Faber, & Horner, 1997). Researchers will often measure advertising appeals or stimuli by isolating a few independent variables and evaluating their impact on dependent measures (e.g., Okechuky & Wang, 1988; Stewart & Furse, 1986; Stewart & Koslow, 1989). This type of research, typically grounded in a specific theoretical framework, examines constructs within that framework to measure (the proposed) advertising effect. Conversely, the term *advertising effectiveness* is defined as the overall contribution to a company or a brand from advertising (Wright-Isak et al., 1997). We can cite one generally accepted premise on the ultimate purpose of advertising: to influence consumer behavior either by changing it or by reinforcing it in the advertisers' best interest (Schreiber, 1990).

The literature includes an array of vast and debatable measures of advertising effectiveness. Professionals have applied many different theories and approaches (Kelley & Turley, 2004). Some would argue for bottom-line measures where effectiveness could represent the return on advertising investment in the form of sales. This type of measure proves highly unrealistic since the relationship tends to be specifically unknown and extremely difficult to quantify (Schreiber & Appel, 1991; Wright-Isak et al., 1997). Other measures of effectiveness include a ratio between market share and market voice (Jones, 1990), the relationship between the content of media and the media in which they appear (Bogart, 1976), and consumer knowledge and belief measures (Schultz, 1990; Wright-Isak et al., 1997). Korgaonkar, Moschis, and Bellenger (1984) surveyed 2,000 advertising agency executives to determine if they viewed a successful advertising campaign as measured in sales, attitude, and awareness measures combined. Successful campaigns were based on marketing research and a solid media plan, financially backed, and tailored with messages perceived as creative and unique.

In addition, the definition of advertising effectiveness can differ depending on whether you ask marketers and syndicated researchers, advertising agencies, or advertising academics. Cook and Kover (1997) found that marketers and syndicated research providers take a very pragmatic approach to effectiveness by linking copy quality, attitude and belief change, media weight, and scheduling to financial result-oriented goals such as sales and profits. On the other hand, advertising agency researchers look at effectiveness as a way to look good to the client and continue to gain new business. Academicians define advertising effectiveness in terms of the language and theories for which they trained, with exact definitions and measures depending on their own particular academic orientation.

Wright-Isak et al. (1997) defined four criteria for demonstrating advertising effectiveness. First, each advertising effort should have a distinct measurable goal. Second, measurement of effectiveness should establish indirect links between advertising's expected impact and the ultimate marketing goals. Third, effectiveness measures should account for the creative idea driving the campaign. Lastly, advertising effectiveness measures should recognize and account for possible carryover and holdover effects, which can affect the brand on a long-term basis (Kotler, 1971; Lechenby & Wedding, 1982; Palda, 1964).

Overall, the profession typically evaluates advertising effectiveness by setting measurable communication objectives based on the human response to the communication. Copy-testing services evaluate the strong and weak points in advertising and test advertising response (Wells et al., 2006). Many advertising agencies outsource their copy-testing to external firms, and these companies use a variety of measurement tests. Huberty (2002) reported on Ameritest, Advertising Research System (ARS), Diagnostic Research, IPSOS-ASI, Mapes & Ross, Millward Brown, and RoperASW, all large and popular copy-testing firms. To measure advertising effectiveness, these firms use items such as:

- Attitude toward the ad
- Brand linkage
- Comprehension
- Feelings toward the ad
- Involvement
- Persuasion of purchase intent or brand switch
- Recall, attention
- Relevance
- Uniqueness

Advertisers often use these copy-testing measures during all stages of a campaign from the developmental research and pre-testing to concurrent or ad-tracking research and finally to post-testing research (Wells et al., 2006).

ARF addressed advertising effectiveness by researching the validity of various copy-testing procedures. Haley and Baldinger (1991) oversaw "The ARF Copy Research Validity Project," which addressed some critical questions on the advertising effectiveness of industry-wide copy-testing measures. The research set out to understand how accurately widely accepted copy-testing measures identified known sales winners. The study examined which individual measures proved best and most predictive, the difference between on-air measures and off-air measures, the difference between pre/post designs and posttest-only design measures, and single and multiple exposure measures. The study set out to conclude, ultimately, the superiority of one method over the rest. One of the primary findings from this rigid and thorough project included the need for companies to use multiple measures when evaluating effectiveness. This finding was substantiated because advertising works at different levels. Results also concluded all commonly employed copy-testing measures such as persuasion, recall, copy playback, and brand salience have predictive validity. Pre/post designs and post-only designs performed well with the exception of the performance of the pre/post design contingent on disguise of dependent measures. Off-air laboratory approaches did well when compared to more realistic commercial viewing settings. Lastly, the findings suggest the need to add likeability to copy-testing measures, since the project found a strong relationship between likeability of the copy and its effects on sales. Regardless of the copy-testing design, these measures tend to address only the mental processes—only one level currently used to evaluate advertising effectiveness.

We can assess the role of advertising and its effectiveness at three levels: inputs, mental processes, and outcomes (Vakratasas & Ambler, 1999; Tellis, 2004). Advertising inputs can be assessed based on intensity, media, and creative content. Inputs include the source part of the communication model. Advertising mental processes measure cognitive, affective, or conative change produced by advertising exposure. Outcome measures gauge behavior such as brand choice, purchase intensity, sales, revenues, or profits (Tellis, 2004).

THEORETICAL MODELS OF ADVERTISING EFFECTIVENESS

Vakratsas and Ambler (1999) reviewed more than 250 academic journal articles and books to summarize the literature regarding intermediate advertising effects. Intermediate effects are defined as measures of consumer attitude and beliefs, purchase intent and/or brand choice measures. The basis of intermediate effects relates importantly to the current study since judges of EFFIE commercial campaigns base their decisions on campaign periods usually spanning 1 to 4 years. In other words, EFFIE awards look specifically at intermediate effects of advertising, since they do not evaluate effects via experimental design, and they do not look at the long-term impact of advertising. Vakratsas and Ambler (1999) summarized their review of the literature into effect taxonomies. They first discuss taxonomy as one of market response. Market response effectiveness models are economic and do not directly link intermediate advertising effects directly to advertising stimuli. This taxonomy concerns itself with measuring advertising weights and correlating weights to aggregate-level marketing measures (Bass & Clark, 1972; Rao, 1986; Little, 1979). The hierarchy-free model comprises another. These models assume no particular processing formula but consider advertising as part of the overall brand totality (Lannon & Cooper, 1983). The remaining taxonomies discussed by Vakratsas and Ambler (1999) examine how the literature states advertising works with cognition effects (Nelson, 1970; Stigler, 1961; Telser, 1964) or affect (Zajonc, 1980), or in a hierarchical combination where brackets or combinations indicate the order of an advertising effect. We refer to these various combination models as *integrative* since the processing is contingent on involvement with the product category (Vakratsas & Ambler, 1999, p. 28).

Hierarchy of Effects Models
Hierarchy models of advertising effects act as persuasive models, with clear indications and flow at each level of the hierarchy. These types of models have played a significant role in the development of advertising research (Vakratsas & Ambler, 1999). In the advertising literature, we find not one single hierarchy model but many different models based on different factors. Many of

these models have a historical framework in the personal-selling literature, adapted later to advertising (Barry, 1987). The first commonly known model, AIDA, stands for attention, interest, desire, and action and came from the works of St. Elmo Lewis (Barry, 1987). This framework gives a step-by-step account of how consumer processing occurs. Many credit the AIDA model with blazing the trail for advertising research frameworks over the next 60 years (Barry & Howard, 1990). Lavidge and Steiner's (1961) work began the modern thread of hierarchy literature. The work of Lavidge and Steiner (1961) represents one of the first to state two important points. Advertising should not be designed to produce immediate purchases, and using sales to measure advertising effectiveness is incomplete and problematic. Lavidge and Steiner (1961) suggested their hierarchy works with components related to the classic psychological model: cognitive, affective, and conative or motivational. The first two steps of the hierarchy, awareness and knowledge, relate to information and tend toward the cognitive. The next two steps, liking and preference, relate more to attitudes and feelings. The last two steps, conviction and purchase, tend toward the motivational. Colley (1961) added to the hierarchy literature by developing DAGMAR: Defining Advertising Goals for Measured Advertising Objectives (Barry, 1987). Based in this groundwork, advertising managers could now set a hierarchy of advertising objectives rather than focusing on sales goals alone (Colley, 1961; Barry & Howard, 1990).

Since the birth of the general hierarchy model, alternative and integrative models have come into existence. Krugman (1965) added to the concept of involvement regarding hierarchy models by citing involvement as the number of linkages between the advertised product and the consumers' experiences. Krugman proposed that a low-involvement hierarchy exists with low consumer involvement in a product category and repetition of advertisements leads to modifying cognitive structures. These modified cognitive structures lead to trial and then feelings regarding the experience. This type of model can be considered cognition-conation-affect.

Zajonc (1980, 1986) and Zajonc and Markus (1982) did not consider cognition required for establishing preferences but more important in the justification of the action. Here, affect represents the driving force, and this hierarchical model can be considered affect-conation-cognition. With this research, consumer behavior researchers began to examine the power of affect as a moderating force in advertising effectiveness.

The review of hierarchy models herein is not intended to be exhaustive, rather serves as the basis for the message strategy models further discussed in this literature review. We should mention that hierarchy of effects models have their critics who consider them over simplistic. Moriarty (1983) found hierarchy of effects models too lock-step and sequential and not representative of the way advertising occurs. Still, most of the models we find in literature today are grounded in a type of hierarchy framework. Collectively, the message-processing models discussed later are persuasive and integrative hierarchy models. These models establish the framework for the commercial message strategies examined herein.

Elaboration Likelihood Model
The elaboration likelihood model (ELM) offers one of the most comprehensive persuasive hierarchical models (Vakratsas & Ambler, 1999). Petty, Cacioppo, and Schumann (1983) proposed central and peripheral routes to advertising effectiveness. They believe different appeals may affect attitude change for different audiences. The model, a dual-processing one, finds different

attitude change based on different degrees of elaborative information processing activity (Petty, Wheeler, & Bizer, 2000). Central route appeals change attitude because of a person's processing of cognitive information relevant to a particular attitudinal position and their motivation to elaborate the information. Central route appeals tend toward the cognitive (Petty et al., 1983; Vakratsas & Ambler, 1999). Peripheral route attitude change occurs through nonelaboration cues where the person pays more attention to the execution elements and not necessarily to the information or argument strength of the message (Petty et al., 1983). However, attitude change is not mutually exclusive to each route of persuasion, and source factors can affect persuasion by both the central and message factors (Petty & Cacioppo, 1984). Consumer involvement mediates the processing and impact of any advertising execution (Petty et al., 1983).

FCB Grid

Vaughn (1980, 1986) presents overview sketches into possible implications from advertising effectiveness theory. According to Vaughn, the greater purpose of the FCB grid gives a better understanding of how to evaluate advertising strategy options and ways of planning, creating, executing, and testing more effective advertising. Vaughn bases the grid on what he considered the four traditional theories of advertising effectiveness prominent in marketing: economic, responsive, psychological, and social. Economic theory considers consumers rational and believes they will act with calculated decision processes. Responsive theory says consumers exert minimal effort and develop habits through stimulus-response learning. Psychological theory represents the basis for ego-driven, decision-making behavior. Social theory describes consumers' actions as persuaded in connection with group roles. The FCB grid derives from Lavidge and Steiner's (1961) "Hierarchy of Effects" and the concept of consumer involvement. Together the theories, hierarchy, and consumer involvement form the four quadrants of the FCB grid.

Vaughn (1980) places on the high end of involvement those decisions high in cost, ego support, social value, or newness, while low-involvement decisions sit at the opposite extreme. The first quadrant involves High (Involvement)/Thinking (Informative), and message strategies should focus on providing information or demonstrations. This quadrant applies to products considered major purchases such as a house, car, or home furnishings. The second quadrant, High (Involvement)/Feeling (Affective) applies when the product relates more to self esteem issues. Hence, heavy information does not seem as important. This quadrant fits well with jewelry, cosmetics, and fashion. The third quadrant, Low (Involvement)/Thinking (Habit Formation) relates to products typically considered habitual or convenience purchases. Strategy for these items focused on creating a point-of-difference to generate positive outcomes. The fourth quadrant Low (Involvement)/Feeling (Self-Satisfaction) involves products satisfying personal cravings or tastes such as candy, cigarettes, beer, and liquor. In the Low/Feeling quadrant, consumer interest is short-lived and creative attention-getting techniques could operate as an effective strategy. Vaughn stated that although this model seems simple, few advertising strategies are simple and products will have varying degrees of movement around their quadrant. This movement can create overlaps in possible strategy decisions. Figure 1 displays the FCB grid.

Ratchford (1987) presented a detailed account of the development, reliability, and validity of the scales used for measuring the location of product categories on the FCB grid. The goal of the grid is to find positions where product categories reside based

FIGURE 1. FCB grid.

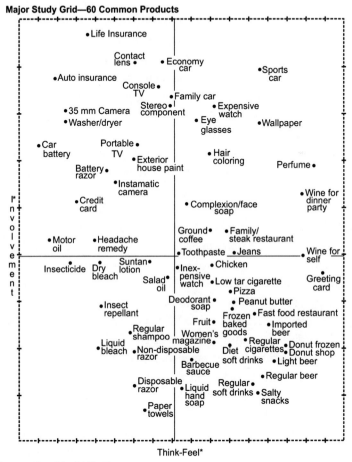

Major Study Grid—60 Common Products

Think-Feel*

Source. Ratchford (1987).
*Numbers are scale values x 100.

on consumer levels of involvement and consumer estimation of the think/feel dimension. Ratchford described the grid as a continuum since thinking and feeling at any level of involvement can occur simultaneously, with products being equal in either category residing in the middle. The FCB scale was developed based on three general notions: (1) internal consistency exhibited by common factor analysis loadings and a satisfactory coefficient alpha, (2) ability to discriminate between products, and (3) respondent understanding. The scales developed over five developmental studies and one final study. As for reliability, internal consistency of product means of .76 was reported in the final study, and results were consistent across studies (Figure 1).

Ratchford (1987) also addressed FCB validity issues. Content validity was appropriate because of consistency of the fit of constructs in relation to previous definitions of involvement, thinking, and feeling as well as through qualitative analysis. However, with trait and discriminant validity assessed using factor analysis, items from involvement and thinking tended to load on the same factor. Ratchford explained this does not exemplify a lack of discriminant validity but a reflection of a hypothesized notion of thinking and feeling as antecedents of involvement. Criterion validity was assessed from the .76 correlations comparing between Zaichkowsky's (1985) measure of involvement and the FCB measure. Predictive validity was demonstrated through a comparison of the multi-dimensional scaling output from studies 2 and 3. In sum, the validation of the measurement and placement of product categories on the FCB grid was substantiated and consistent with previous studies measuring the constructs used.

Rossiter–Percy Grid
The FCB model does have its critics who say it oversimplifies the advertising planning decision processes. Rossiter, Percy,

and Donovan (1991) proposed a practical and theoretically improved grid called the Rossiter-Percy grid (RP grid). Rossiter et al. (1991) argued for a more valid connection between product and advertising strategy. Overall, their grid differs in that it attempts to acknowledge more accurately not only differences in product category but also differences in brands. Differences in brands, even in the same product category can have different brand-purchase motivations. Rossiter et al. (1991) refer to the FCB grid and the RP grid as essentially models of attitude representations of how consumers evaluate products and brands.

Rossiter et al. (1991) considered their first improvement over the FCB grid the addition of the concept of brand awareness as a necessary communication objective. Rossiter et al. explain, "Brand attitude without prior brand awareness is an insufficient advertising communication objective. The fundamental advertising communication objectives are to maximize brand attitude given brand awareness (that is, to maximize brand attitude conditional on the prior establishment of brand awareness)" (p. 12). The RP model breaks brand awareness into two categories: brand recognition and brand recall. When recognition represents a specific communication objective, Rossiter et al. suggested promoting visual displays of packaging and/or the brand. When brand recall becomes more important, creative executions should encourage associative learning (Allen & Janiszewski, 1989) between the brand and product category. Rossiter et al. believe the FCB grid inadequately addresses the construct of involvement and confounds product category and brand involvement. The RP grid improves the involvement dimension by defining involvement simply as perceived risk with the brand and the audience's knowledge of the brand within the product category.

Rossiter et al. (1991) found the overall lack of accountability regarding consumer purchase motivation another drawback of the FCB grid. The RP grid addresses this void by attaching motives to the original think and feel dimensions found in the FCB model. Think motives, more specifically defined as informational motives negatively reinforcing purchase motivations, include: problem removal, problem avoidance, incomplete satisfaction, mixed approach-avoidance, and normal depletion. The RP grid calls feel motives transformational motives or positively reinforcing motives. According to Rossiter et al. (1991, p. 16) transformational motives "promise to enhance the brand user by effecting a transformation in the brand user's sensory, mental, or social state." These motives include: sensory gratification, intellectual stimulation, and social approval. This negative and positive motivation distinction represents a critical difference between the FCB grid and the RP grid since this distinction is vital to formulating effective message tactics. In addition, the RP grid addresses the need to include social approval motivation, which the FCB grid does not address. Ratchford (1987) stated the FCB grid did not include this dimension because respondents said they did not make decisions based on what others think.

Lastly, Ratchford (1987) reported analysis while building the FCB grid found a high positive correlation between involvement and the thinking dimension, dismissing the finding because of the assumption that when consumers think carefully about a decision it makes them more involved, while actions based on feelings alone would not carry the same involvement. Rossiter et al. (1991) state this assumption omits high-involvement transformational products.

Rossiter et al. (1991) say the FCB grid offers no real model for designing advertising tactics. However, through the RP grid, examples of advertising tactics are offered reflecting the fact that all advertisements represent a balance between rational and emotional, as well as positive and negative stimuli, in ads. For example, low-involvement/informational brand attitude strategies should use a simple problem-solution format, include one or two benefits, state benefit claims explicitly, and be easy to learn in one or two exposures. The audience does not have to like the ad prepared for low-involvement/informational products. For low involvement, transformational brand strategies, emotional authenticity with a single benefit should be the key element. Emotion execution must be unique to the brand and the audience must like the ad. Rossiter et al. found consistency here with the RP grid and Lutz, MacKenzie, and Belch (1983), who considered attitude toward the ad a necessary mediator for attitude toward the brand. Also, implicit associations and repetition serve as reinforcement functions for low-involvement transformational advertising. Advertising tactics for high-involvement informational-brand-attitude strategies include:

- Correct emotional portrayals
- Convincing benefit claims
- Avoiding exaggerations
- Possible competitive/refutable approaches with competition or if objections to the brand exist

The RP grid brand-attitude strategies for high-involvement transformational tactics should include authentic emotional portrayals tailored to the target audience lifestyle and communication that assists in linking personal identification with the product. Additional high-involvement transformational strategies should utilize repetition as a brand-building and reinforcement function.

Although the RP grid addresses many of the drawbacks of the FCB grid, Rossiter et al. (1991) provide no thorough strategy-grid structure allowing a researcher to assign products/brands into quadrants such as those of the FCB grid. This relates pragmatically to the current research since hypotheses will be formed based on where products reside in relation to the think/feel quadrants of the FCB grid. Although advertising textbooks discuss the FCB grid and RP grid, these models suffer from a significant paucity of published research testing them.

Regardless of the advertising planning grid used, Berger (1986) hypothesized the general trend in advertising will move more toward feeling motives because of the degree of sameness found in products as more products enter a specific product category. This homogeny in products causes advertisers to differentiate through image and emotional strategies.

MESSAGE STRATEGIES AND TYPOLOGIES

Frazer (1983) defined creative strategy as, "a policy or guiding principle which specifies the general nature and character of messages to be designed. Strategy states the means selection to achieve the desired audience effect over the term of the campaign" (p. 36). Frazer considered the emphasis of strategy rests not on the specific message tactics but on the overall guiding principles applicable to all areas of the promotional mix. His theoretical contribution proposed creative strategy taxonomies, defining seven creative strategy alternatives:

- Anomalous/affective
- Brand image
- Generic
- Positioning
- Preemptive
- Resonance
- Unique selling proposition

Generic strategies make a claim all brands in the product category can make. Preemptive strategies highlight a specific product or service point common to all products, but do it in a way the specific point sounds inherent to the advertised product. Unique selling propositions focus on a unique consumer benefit. Brand-image strategies associate images, social situations, and symbols with the brand and tend to appeal to consumers psychologically. Positioning strategy gives the product a unique place in the consumer's mind, a strategy well suited for new entries or brands with small market share. Resonance strategy seeks to display experiences of the consumer, imagined or otherwise, with those portrayed in the advertisement to create a relationship. Anomalous/affective strategy attempts to connect directly to the consumer's emotions.

Informational and Transformational Messages
Resnik and Stern (1977) analyzed information content in television commercials based on information cues and dayparts (time of airing) to evaluate the use of informative content. To be considered informative, a television commercial must aid the consumer in making a better decision compared to the decision they would have made prior to exposure. Informative cues include:

- Availability
- Contents or components
- Guarantees or warrantees
- New ideas
- Nutrition
- Packaging
- Price or value
- Quality/performance
- Research

- Safety
- Special offers
- Taste

Based on an observation of 378 television commercials, less than half of the total sample contained one informational element, and less than 35% of the commercials during the weekend mornings and weekday afternoons contained one element. Findings concluded advertising for institutions, toys, hobbies, and transportation proved more informative while advertisements for food, personal care, laundry, and household products contained less informative cues. In addition, weekday mornings and evenings had a 60% proportion of informative commercials. The authors declare this study purposely avoided considering image or psychologically related appeals as informative ones.

Puto and Wells (1984) proposed a theoretical structure for advertising effects based on informational and transformational advertising. We judge advertising informational if it contains factual and verifiable information about the brand important to the consumer. Informational advertising has theoretical framework in information processing concepts of consumer behavior (Bettman, 1979; Fishbein & Ajzen, 1975). Transformational advertising displays the experience of using the product in an exciting or enjoyable manner, and this very specific connection causes the consumer to recall the brand with the experience. Transformational advertising is based on emotion (Clynes, 1980; Rogers, 1983), vicarious classical conditioning (Berger, 1962; Petty & Cacioppo, 1981), and motivational research (Dichter, 1964). Based on this theoretical framework, Puto and Wells (1984) built a measurement scale to distinguish these two dimensions.

Laskey, Day, and Crask (1989) established a classification method and scheme of message typologies building off the research of Wells (1980), Fraser (1983), Aaker and Norris (1982), Vaughn (1980), Rossiter and Percy (1987), and Puto and Wells (1984). The method employs a two-step coding approach. They explain the two-step approach as essential for addressing the detailed classification schemes coders face when content analyzing commercials. The first step is to identify the message as informational or transformational. The informational message, "provides consumers with factual (i.e., presumably verifiable), relevant brand data in a clear and logical manner such that they have greater confidence in their ability to assess the merits of buying the brand after having seen the advertisement" (Laskey et al., 1989, p. 38). The transformational message, "associates the experience of using (consuming) the advertised brand with a unique set of psychological characteristics which would not typically be associated with the brand experience to the same degree without exposure to the [advertising]" (Laskey et al., 1989, p. 38).

The second typology coding step classifies the messages into subcategories corresponding to the initial classification schema. Informational subcategories include: comparative, unique selling proposition (USP), preemptive, hyperbole, and generic-informational. The first informational subcategory, comparative advertising, shows or mentions competing brands. Laskey et al. (1989) stated this comparative strategy derives from Frazer's (1983) positioning strategy. The USP informational strategy uses claims of uniqueness as the primary focus of the advertisement. These claims of uniqueness must involve proven product attribute or benefit-in-use factors and must not include subjective claims. The preemptive strategy, borrowed from Frazer (1983) involves a brand characteristic common to all brands in the product category but highlighted by only one of the brands as a way to differentiate. In a preemptive strategy, a brand communicates ownership of a common characteristic found among all competing brands such as Folgers saying their coffee is "mountain grown." However, Laskey et al. (1989) found coders had a difficult time distinguishing between USP and preemptive message strategies. To overcome this difficulty, Laskey et al. (1989) stated preemptive advertisements should contain no indication of uniqueness or mention of competitive brands. The hyperbole-informational strategy has the appearance of being factually based but actually builds on exaggerated claims. Lastly, the generic-informational strategy focuses on the product class more so than the actual brand name.

We classify overall transformational advertisements by using transformational subtypes: user image, brand image, use occasion, and generic-transformational. User image messages focus on the users of the brand instead of the brand itself. This category resembles Frazer's (1983) resonance category. Laskey et al. (1989) found the user-image category often used for beer and wine products, personal care products, office products, and clothing, with the focus on the lifestyle of the user. In contrast, brand-image commercials attempt to convey the brand's personality, often attributing status, luxury, prestige, and quality directly to the brand. The focus here is on the brand and not the user of the brand. The use-occasion-transformational category displays situations of brand use, building an association of use occasion and experience. Lastly, similar to the generic-informational, the generic-transformational message uses a generic approach appealing to transformational motives with message strategies focused on product class not brand specific.

Laskey et al. (1989) tested their typology by content analyzing 900 commercials supplied by Research Systems Corporation of Evansville, Indiana. Commercials included a wide range of package goods. Laskey and Crask (1990) used the typology classification definitions to present a decision model for managers regarding the appropriateness or compatibility of using a particular message strategy based on a previously designed positioning strategy.

Laskey, Fox, and Crask (1995) examined empirically the relationship between television commercial effectiveness and message strategy with three overall research goals:

1. Determine if informational or transformational differed relative to effectiveness
2. Evaluate the effectiveness of the subcategories found in the two main message strategy groups
3. Evaluate effectiveness of message strategies by product category

Recall, key message comprehension, and persuasion measures evaluated effectiveness. Dependent measures of effectiveness were evaluated by using the Advertising Research System (ARS). The study examined 1,178 commercials including 336 brands, with at least 50 different brands and 10 different manufacturers included in each product category. Products were placed in five main categories:

- Breakfast foods and snacks
- Entrees and side dishes
- Household items
- Over-the-counter (OTC) products
- Personal care items

The aggregate results between informational and transformational message strategies indicated no significant differences in persuasion or recall measures. However, informational messages did differ significantly in message comprehension measures. Examination of specific subcategories found no significant differences in effectiveness measures for transformational advertisements. For informational advertisements, the unique selling proposition yielded positive advantages while the hyperbole strategy yielded negative advantages in persuasion measures. The analysis of product category groups yielded eight significant relationships with various effectiveness measures. For the breakfast food category, hyperbole related negatively and preemptive related positively to persuasion measures. Comparative and USP both related negatively to recall. For OTC products, USP produced negative results in key message comprehension measurement. For household items, persuasion scores significantly increased with USP message strategies but significantly decreased with hyperbole. Comparison advertising strategy produced negative results in key message comprehension.

Laskey, Fox, and Crask (1994) examined the relationship between television executional style, as defined by Shimp's (1974) typologies and commercial effectiveness as well as identifying whether they differ across product categories. The dependent measures of effectiveness included recall, key message comprehension, and persuasion (see Stewart & Furse, 1986). They used the identical sample of commercials as Laskey et al. (1995), with 1,178 television ads consisting of 336 different brands divided into five product categories. Results indicated no significant advantages or disadvantages to any particular style in persuasion score measures. Six executional styles affected recall measures. Typical person endorser, spokesperson, and fantasy had a positive recall impact while narration, demonstration, and display had a negative recall impact. Only two executional styles affected key-message comprehension. The typical person endorser had positive key-message impact, while the display style had negative key-message impact. As for impact of executional style by product category, none significantly improved or reduced persuasion measures, but various findings for related recall and key-message comprehension were reported. For entrees and side dishes, only the spokesperson style produced a positive improvement for related recall and key-message comprehension. For personal-care items, the typical person endorser created significantly more positive results, while display formats produced significantly more negative results for related recall and key-message comprehension. In addition, on-camera video dramas produced significantly higher key-message comprehension scores. For household items, the typical person endorser and fantasy executional deliveries produced more positive results, while demonstration and display styles produced negative-related recall results. Lastly, typical person endorser styles produced more positive key-message comprehension scores for OTC products.

Laskey et al. (1994) also examined the frequency of styles within product categories and found some styles used more often than others. For breakfast foods, the celebrity endorser ranked high while spokesperson, off-camera dramas, and demonstrations did not. For the entrees and side dishes category, only the demonstration style occurred less often than others. Fantasy occurred less often in the personal-care items product category. In the household item category, spokesperson, demonstration, and fantasy formats presented more often, while celebrity endorser, off-camera video drama, and display ranked least popular. Conversely, off-camera video dramas were more common and demonstration and fantasy were less popular in the OTC category.

Ramaprasad and Hasegawa (1992) used Laskey et al. (1989) message typologies for comparing American and Japanese television commercials. Ramaprasad and Hasegawa's (1992) findings resembled Laskey et al.'s (1989) results. However, the study did find less use of comparative informational strategy and hyperbole in Japanese commercials and more use of preemptive and USP.

Yssel and Gustafson (1998) employed the message typology developed by Laskey et al. (1989) to analyze strategic message designs manifest in Leo Burnett's reel, *The 100 Best Commercials Ever Made Around the World.* This was produced internally by advertising professionals at Leo Burnett. Their analysis classified 62% of the commercials as transformational advertising strategies compared to 30% classified as informational ones. Of the informational strategies, 44% were classified as preemptive and 33% were classified as USP. Brand image dominated the transformational classifications.

Taylor Six-Segment Strategy Wheel
Taking the literature one large step further, Taylor (1999) designed the "Six-segment Message Strategy Wheel." His conceptual model draws upon much of the literature's message strategy theoretical framework. Taylor's work captures Kotler's summary of social science literature, Vaughn's FCB grid, Petty and Cacioppo's ELM framework, Frazer's creative strategy summary, and Laskey et al.'s typology of main message strategies for television commercials. Taylor divided his model into six segments. The first segment, called the Freudian Psychoanalytic Model, applies when the consumer needs to make a personal, ego-related statement. The second segment, called the Veblenian social-psychological model, comes into play when the consumer requires the product to make a statement to others. Cyrenaics, the third segment, involves products that stimulate the five senses. The fourth segment, the Pavlovian learning model, represents products that typically fall into habitual purchases patterns for consumers. The fifth segment,

the acute need model, captures the consumer's need for a high-involvement product decision based on limited time resources. The sixth segment, the Marshallian economic model, assumes a rational and conscious consumer requiring a large amount of information prior to making a purchase decision. Taylor (1999) tested the theoretical model with a one-page, self-administered questionnaire given to 178 respondents. The six-segment message strategy wheel did demonstrate consistency as to how people make buying decisions.

Hwang, McMillian, and Lee (2005) used Taylor's (1999) strategy wheel to investigate the corporate Web site as a corporate advertisement. Using content analysis, three coders analyzed 160 corporate Web sites, and they found sites address multiple audiences within a single site. Messages strategies were mainly based in information, but high-revenue companies were more likely than low-revenue companies to use transformational messages. Although not theoretically tested here, Taylor's (1999) model is important to mention because of its contribution to the literature.

EXECUTIONAL ELEMENTS AND TACTICS IN COMMERCIALS

In addition to message strategy typologies, we will explore an examination of executional or tactical devices found in television advertisements from effective campaigns. Strategy can be differentiated through tactical elements (Frazer et al., 2002). Commercial features are important, and different effective formulas may exist in different types of commercials. Furthermore, a finite number of executional characteristics exists, which, if reliably coded, could help identify characteristics of advertising effectiveness (McEwen & Leavitt, 1976). An inventory of tactics is important since the groupings of facts, observations, classifying endeavors, and the examination of empirical relationships in totality can make theory realistically possible (Kuhn, 1970).

Stewart and Furse—A Study of 1,000 Commercials

Stewart and Furse (1986) developed a coding methodology for examining the executional factors of television advertising. Their very detailed and thorough study examined how different executional variables related positively or negatively to the advertising-effectiveness-dependent performance measures of recall, key message comprehension, and persuasion. Their coding instrument consisted of 155 items including the following executional elements:

- Auditory devices
- Commercial appeals/selling propositions
- Commercial format
- Commercial structure
- Comparisons
- Setting
- Timing/counting measures
- Tone
- Use of characters
- Use of music
- Visual devices

A professional copy-testing organization collected their data using a sample of 1,059 commercials collected from 1980 to 1983. The sample contained 356 nondurable brands from 115 product categories represented by 63 advertising firms.

The study found brand-differentiating messages served as the single most important factor for explaining dependent-recall and persuasion-measure variation. However, it also addressed many other results regarding the relationship between executional elements and advertising-effectiveness-dependent measures. Examples of factors negatively related to advertising recall included:

- Direct comparisons with competitors
- Graphic displays
- Information on components/ingredients
- Information on nutrition/health
- Research information
- Substantive supers

Examples of factors positively related to advertising recall included:

- Brand-differentiating messages
- Cute/humorous commercial tone
- Fantasy/surreal formats
- Information on convenience of use
- Memorable rhyme/mnemonic device
- Product use and results
- Puffery

Executional elements negatively related to persuasion measures included:

- Information on ingredients
- Information on nutrition
- Male principle character or background cast

- Outdoor setting
- Psychological appeals

Factors positively related to persuasion measures included:

- Brand-differentiating message
- Demonstration format
- Humor
- Indirect comparisons to competitors
- Information on convenience of use
- New product features
- No principle characters
- Product performance/benefit

Stewart and Koslow (1989) used the same methodology as Stewart and Furse (1986) to examine another set of television advertisements. The authors felt they could enhance the power of the original findings if they replicated the results using a different set of commercials produced at a different time. Similar findings resulted with the presence of a brand-differentiating message being the most important variance explaining factor.

Garnard and Morris (1988) studied Clio-winning television advertising ($N = 121$) from 1975 to 1985, in terms of Stewart and Furse's (1986) coding instrument and compared their findings to those of Stewart and Furse on the basis of representation proportions. They discovered many differences compared to the Stewart and Furse (1986) findings. According to their study, some of the characteristics from what their data reported as the ideal Clio commercial would include:

- Animals
- Children in major or minor roles

- Comedy/overall humorous tone
- Continuity of action
- Enjoyment and psychological benefits
- Focus on a single product
- Indoor setting
- Main actor as ordinary person
- Male character in a leading role with a background cast
- Minorities absent
- Music used to create a mood
- Positive emotional appeal
- Product benefits as a featured element
- Strong front-end impact with a blind lead-in
- Overall tone of humor
- Visual and auditory brand sign-offs

Frazer et al. (2002) combined the research elements of message strategy (Frazer, 1983; Laskey et al., 1989) as well as execution elements included in Stewart and Furse (1986). Specifically, they compared EFFIE award-winning advertising found in the United States with Australian advertising in regard to the types of promises, appeals and selling propositions, commercial tone, approach (rational or emotional and positive or negative), and the existence of a brand-differentiating message. They discovered creative strategies represented the greatest differences between the two countries. They found informational strategies chosen in 70% of the U.S. advertisements with informational and transformational advertisements evenly split in Australia. Commercials from both countries had strong links to product performance information, such as attributes and ingredients. Almost half of the total commercial sample featured a product-performance appeal. Humor appeared as the predominate tone in 40% of the U.S. EFFIE winners.

RESEARCH QUESTIONS

The goal of this research, to explore the message strategies and devices found in commercials from effective campaigns (EFFIE), will also evaluate how these characteristics fit into current theoretical advertising strategies. This research will also examine theoretically the congruency of products found on the FCB grid with the think/feel dimensions of the FCB grid based on a comparison with the informational and transformational Laskey's et al. (1989) message strategies. We study the degree to which we can predict message strategies by product placement on the FCB grid. We expect that advertisers will use informational message strategies for think-type products and transformational product strategies for feel-type products. We also investigate trends and differences in message and execution strategy between informational and transformational advertisements. Message strategies establish the basic framework of the message itself and usually serve as the starting point for the development of any creative execution (Frazer et al., 2002; Laskey, et al. 1989). While message strategies establish the guidelines, devices or executional elements comprise the components of the message itself (Stewart & Furse, 1986; Stewart & Koslow, 1989). This research will focus on understanding the manifest and latent characteristics of EFFIE advertisements as well as examine differences compared to the findings of Stewart and Furse (1986). Based on the previous literature review, we propose the following research questions and predictions:

Prediction 1: *Advertisements for product categories on the FCB grid as thinking products will exhibit more informational message strategies than transformational message strategies.*

Prediction 2: *Advertisements for products categorized on the FCB grid as feeling products will exhibit more transformational message strategies than informational message strategies.*

Research Question 1: *What trends have occurred over time regarding informational and transformational message strategies found in EFFIE award-winning campaigns?*

Research Question 2: *Do certain product categories have consistent message typologies over time?*

Research Question 3: *What are the significant differences in executional characteristics between informational and transformational EFFIE television advertisements?*

Research Question 4: *What trends have occurred over time regarding executional factors found in EFFIE award-winning commercials?*

Research Question 5: *Were there effective executional characteristic proportional differences between Stewart and Furse commercials and EFFIE commercials?*

CHAPTER 3

METHODOLOGY

Content analysis, the study of the message itself and not the communicator or the audience (Kassarjian, 1977), serves as the most appropriate method with which to address this study's hypotheses and research questions. Content analysis allows the researcher to observe and evaluate all forms of recorded communications in a systematic fashion (Kolbe & Burnett, 1991). The method can measure words, symbols, themes, characters, and items, as well as space-and-time measures (Kassarjian, 1977). Riffe, Lacy, and Fico (1998) considered content analysis a replicable examination of communication symbols and a deductive approach to inquiry using predetermined categories to explore research questions and hypotheses. Quantitative content analysis assigns numeric values to content, which allows for numeric descriptions and statistical inference. Content analysis offers an unobtrusive way to collect data and can provide a way to test theory empirically and to generate new research evidence and ideas (Kolbe & Burnett, 1991).

Studies using content analysis have examined advertising, marketing, journalism, and international business in numerous journals, conference proceedings, theses, and dissertations (Abernethy & Franke, 1996). For example, advertising studies have used it to examine such items as gender (Browne, 1998; Ford, Voli, Houneycutt, & Casey, 1998; Maynard & Taylor, 1999), and international advertising (Albers-Miller & Stafford, 1999; Al-Olayan & Kirande, 2000; Ji & McNeal, 2001; Taylor & Stern, 1997). Content analysis has been applied to print (Albers-Miller & Stafford, 1999; Al-Olayan & Kirande; Ford et al., 1998; Huhmann & Brotherton, 1997; Maynard & Taylor, 1999) as well as television content (Alexander, Benjamin, Hoerrner, & Roe, 1998; Browne; Gagnard & Morris, 1988; Ji & McNeal; Stewart & Furse, 1986, 2000; Stewart & Koslow, 1989; Taylor & Stern; Wyatt, McCullough, & Wolgemuth, 1998).

CONTENT ANALYSIS DEFINED

Quantitative content analysis is the objective, systematic, and replicable analysis of manifest and latent content. This cohesive definition comes from combining aspects of definitions provided by authors Berelson (1952), Holsti (1969), Kassarjian (1977), Krippendorff (1980), Kolbe and Burnett (1991), and Riffe et al. (1998). Objectivity establishes the process for which categories are developed and defined. Objective definitions are the basis for the manifest and latent content being examined and/or theoretically tested. In quantitative content analysis, objectivity should be established by previously defined theoretical constructs and operationalized as variables for later descriptive relationship analysis. Rules are then established to govern defined categories as well as data collection methods. These rules are transferable to other studies making the content analysis method systematic. Because the heart of any rigorous content analysis focuses on remaining objective and systematic, the analysis can and should be replicable. Furthermore, with the focus of content analysis on communication content and replicable, content analysis tends to be a good technique for both cross-sectional and longitudinal analysis (Kang, Kara, Laskey, & Seaton, 1993). We use content analysis methods and instruments established from previous studies (Laskey et al., 1989; Stewart & Furse, 1986) to examine television commercials from award-winning EFFIE campaigns.

Previous Television Commercial
Content Analyses Methods
An initial review of previous television advertising studies was done prior to establishing the exact method for the current study to increase the reliability of findings. These studies use the television commercial as the unit of analysis and use many of the same variables we have employed. However, content analysis methods in these studies greatly differ as to how they assigned judges and compute intercoder reliability; two aspects central to rigorous content analysis.

Stewart and Furse (1986) serves as the most referenced source for this research. Their operational definitions and findings form the basis for this research. They employed four coders for all nontiming categories (we use no timing variables in this study). Each coder reviewed each commercial. Majority agreement determined judgments. When agreement reached a 50-50 split, a missing value was assigned. After all coding was completed, only reliabilities of .60 or higher were used in the analysis. Reliabilities were obtained for nondichotomous categorical variables by computing a contingency coefficient. Stewart and Koslow (1989) followed this same methodology.

Laskey et al. (1989) used five coders to review each commercial and each coder reviewed commercials independently. Laskey et al. set the criterion that four out of five coders must agree. They used a contingency coefficient similar to Stewart and Furse (1986) to report reliability resulting in a .94 contingency coefficient for informational and transformational classification and .90 contingency coefficient for subcategory message strategy classification. Overall, Laskey et al. (1989) arrived at an average contingency coefficient of .897 by calculating the agreement for each pair of coders and then averaging across categories. Laskey, Fox, and Crask (1994, 1995) also used the four-out-of-five agreement criterion, but deviated from the contingency coefficient by using the Krippendorff (1980) alpha coefficient for reliability reporting.

Other studies examining the television commercial as the unit of analysis used various alternative methods for attaining reliability and studies differed by the amount of reliability information they reported. Ramaprasad and Hasegawa (1992) did not report the number of coders used in the study but did report using Holsti's (1969) formula for computing reliability. They coded a sub-sample of 10% of the total sample commercials to arrive at a figure to report as reliability. Gagnard and Morris (1988) used three coders to examine Clio advertisements and also used the Holsti (1969) formula for the reporting of intercoder reliability. However, Gagnard and Morris (1988) did not report their method of collecting the intercoder sample or how they assigned the coders. Frazer et al. (2002) coded a sample of EFFIE commercials using two coders reporting perfect agreement. Perfect agreement resulted when coders resolved discrepancies through discussion. Kelley and Turley (2004), Alexander et al. (1998), as well as Browne (1998) also resolved their coder disagreements through discussion after computing initial reliabilities. How these studies differ in terms of using a consistent content analysis method becomes problematic. However, this situation is not limited to the scope of the current unit of analysis but can be found across other units and disciplines.

Within the framework of communication research, Riffe and Freitag (1997) examined content analysis studies in terms of frequency, authorship, focus on different media, sampling, theory linking, and reliability. They took their sample frame from the *Journalism and Mass Communication Quarterly*, from 1971 through 1995; finding 24.6% (486 full-length articles) out of the total 1,977 published articles used content analysis. Analysis of newspapers (46.7%) was the most common examined media, with television (24.3%) analyses also taking a large percentage of research interest. Of all the research articles they examined, they found only slightly over one-fourth (27.6%) of the studies linked to theory building, and just under one half (45.7%) used research questions or hypothesis to guide research design. Furthermore, only half of the studies reported intercoder reliability levels with all but a few citing only one overall reliability figure. In other words, there emerged no one conclusive way to insure a proper application of content analysis method to a research problem.

ESTABLISHING THE CURRENT CONTENT ANALYSIS METHOD

To address the previously mentioned methodological inconsistencies, we will implement research proposed by Kassarjian (1977) and Kolbe and Burnett (1991). Kassarjian created an exposition for improving content analysis methodology in the areas of objectivity, systematization, quantification, sampling, and reliability. Kolbe and Burnett (1991) called his work a methodological benchmark. Perhaps Kassarjian's most important contribution came in the area of improving method reliability. He said, "the researcher's subjectivity must be minimized to obtain a systematic, objective description of communication content, the issue of reliability becomes paramount" (p. 14). Intercoder (or interjudge) reliability is critical to any content analysis study because it becomes a basis for analysis quality (Kassarjian; Krippendorff, 1980; Perreault & Leigh, 1989; Kolbe & Burnett).

According to Kassarjian (1977), focus on reliability issues in content analysis tends to revolve around the areas of category reliability and interjudge reliability. Category reliability involves strictly defined, as well as understood, categories which transfer to other studies and generate similar, if not identical, results among judges reviewing the same content. Interjudge reliability is a statistical measure of agreement between several judges processing identical communication content. Both represent extremely important points when addressing manifest, and perhaps more importantly, latent content issues. Differences in meaning can occur with both, and to minimize differences, latent content analysis requires a strictly defined framework for researchers to follow. Riffe et al. (1998) believe manifest and latent content best considered as existing on a continuum because many manifest symbols keep the same meaning over time, while latent symbols can often change either by group association or in other ways over time. Addressing this complexity is essential to creating reliable categories and agreement among judges.

Addressing Category and Interjudge Reliability
Based on the framework proposed by Kassarjian (1977), Kolbe and Burnett (1991) empirically reviewed and synthesized 128

articles from 28 journals, 3 proceedings, and 1 anthology to assess the methods of published content analysis research, as well as to examine their reliability criteria. Their framework analyzed each level of Kassarjian's content analysis definition, and we will use a review of the findings from their analysis to establish the framework for the current study.

For objectivity, Kolbe and Burnett (1991) asked if studies reported: coding rules and procedures, judge training, pretesting measures, the nature of the judges, and if judges worked independently of one another. The authors found 71% of the studies in their sample contained rules and procedures including category details and operational definitions. Only 40.6% of the studies reported judge training. However, Kolbe and Burnett suggested this probably did not mean the judges had no training but that the studies' authors failed to report training. As for pretesting, only 29.7% of the studies reported pretesting measures and/or procedures. Kolbe and Burnett (1991) indicated lack of pretesting as a possible methodological weakness and recommended addressing it during any scientific research.

They also measured judge independence and number of judges. We cannot overstate the importance of judge independence. Overall interjudge reliability measures are based on the systematic and consistent nature of defined variables, and the very basis of reliability is in the foundation of category definitions as well as how well judges agree on content decisions. Kolbe and Burnett (1991) reported only 48.4% of the studies clearly stated the use of independent judges. The number of judges reported from their sample varied. The most frequently reported method used two coders, but the authors state two could be an overestimation of coders who actually coded the main sample. Many studies include reliability coders into the coder total when, in reality, the number of judges who actually coded the data used in the analysis could be less. Overall, 1.6% of the studies reported the use of a single judge, 38.3% used two judges, 30.4% used three or more judges, and 29.7% did not report the number of judges.

The calculation and reporting of reliability is essential to scientifically valid content analysis. Kolbe and Burnett (1991) looked at the reporting of reliability in content analysis studies in two ways: the reliability index used and how the reliability index was reported. Regarding reliability index use, they found the coefficient of agreement in 32% of the articles, and this was the most frequently used reliability index. The coefficient of agreement simply equals the total number of agreements divided by the total number of coding decisions. In addition, 7% of the articles used Krippendorf's alpha, 3.1% used Holsti, and 7.8% used various others. However, no reliability coefficient was reported in 31.3% of the content analyses surveyed. Hughes and Garrett (1990) found a similar result in their content analysis of content analyses found in the *Journal of Consumer Research*, *Journal of Marketing Research* and *Journal of Marketing* spanning from 1984 through 1987. Over 65% of the 86 articles in the sample evaluated reliability with a simple coefficient of agreement. Other methods found that adjust for chance agreement and are applicable to nominal data included Scott's pi (2.3%) and Krippendorff's alpha (1.1%). The proper application and use of a reliability statistic is important to communicate research quality.

Kolbe and Burnett (1991) considered the reporting of the reliability index for each category also important since reporting an overall reliability can lead to misleading results. The authors found 35.9% of the studies only reported an overall measure while 24.2% reported individual measures, and 8.6 simply mentioned a range. Misleading reliability results occur when reporting one aggregate average. Categories with high reliability tend to skew low individual measures. To remedy this situation, the reporting of individual category reliabilities becomes a preferred method.

Overall, Kolbe and Burnett (1991) conclude, "The results indicate that there are a number of gaps in the methods and procedures used by analysts in the areas of objectivity and reliability. Since these two areas are at the heart of content-analysis research and directly affect research quality, the seriousness of the problem becomes evident" (p. 249). Other studies (Kelley & Turley, 2004; Maher & Childs, 2003) have utilized Kolbe and Burnett to improve reliability and stay consistent with literature. The current study uses the Kolbe and Burnett analysis as a research design model to improve where others have varied. Kolbe and Burnett admit their comments may seem a bit idealistic. However, we will apply their review of Kassarjian's (1977) framework—coding rules and procedures, judge training, pretest measures, nature of judges, judge independence, and the detailed reporting of reliability estimates—to the current study to improve reliabilities as well as the overall rigor of this research.

SAMPLE

Commercials used in this analysis come from the EFFIE Awards representing award-winning EFFIE campaigns spanning 1995 through 2004 ($N = 670$). According to research done by Kolbe and Burnett (1991), 39.1% of published content analysis studies have 600 or more units. The initial EFFIE sample frame represents over 40 product categories, 200 advertising agencies, and

300 brands. The available EFFIE commercials were purchased from the AMA in New York City.

CURRENT CODING PROCEDURE AND RELIABILITY ANALYSIS

Adhering to the Kolbe and Burnett (1991) study to improve content analysis objectivity and reliability, we will address the following criteria individually: rules and procedures, including coding instrument and codebook; judge training; pretesting; judge independence; number of judges; and the statistical evaluation of reliability.

Rules and Procedures

Addressing rules and procedures involves a discussion of category details and operational definitions. Kang et al. (1993, p. 18) appropriately summarized coding categories in advertising research, "In advertising applications, concepts of advertising content elements are operationalized through the development of content typologies. To develop a typology, dimensions of advertising content are first identified and then categories within each dimension are established." All dimensions and categories operationalized in this study are identical to the ones discussed in the literature review (Stewart & Furse, 1986; Laskey et al., 1989). Coders (or judges) received a six-page coding instrument for each spot, as well as a codebook addressing operational definitions for each variable in each category. The coding instrument included 61 total categories. The categories chosen for examination were either descriptive information about each spot or categories borrowed from the previous studies discussed in the literature review (with the exception of the hero coding as well as music artist/song known and music style). Categories can be summed up in four different areas.

The first consists of descriptive spot information collected from each EFFIE spot:

- Ad title
- Agency name
- Award level
- Award year
- Brand name
- Coder initials
- Product category
- Spot time
- Use of color film

The second group of variables was the coding framework adapted from Stewart and Furse (1986, pp. 131–143). Many other studies examining television commercials have used various parts of this coding framework (Frazer, Bartel, & Patti, 2002; Gagnard & Morris, 1988; Stewart & Furse, 1986; Stewart & Koslow, 1989), including:

- Auditory devices
- Commercial appeal/selling proposition
- Commercial approach
- Commercial characters
- Commercial format

The third section of the coding framework applied the message typologies and subcategories first used by Laskey et al. (1989, p. 38) and further used in follow-up studies (Frazer et al., 2002; Laskey et al., 1989, 1995; Ramapradasad & Hasegawa, 1992; Yssel & Gustafson, 1998) to examine message strategy. The last typology incorporated in the coding sheet includes the documentation of the presence of a situation when the main character in the spot is/becomes the hero or if the brand is/becomes the hero. (We added this section for future research possibilities and will not discuss findings from these categories in this research.) Lastly, we assigned all category definitions numeric values for later nominal data analysis (Riffe et al., 1998). Appendix A contains a complete copy of the coding instrument.

Judges received instructions to code commercials based on the dominant variable of the specific category manifest in the commercial, choosing variables only if the variable ranked as the dominant choice. We asked judges to use their best judgment to identify the most dominant trait, even when other traits were present. If no clear dominant trait emerged, judges were asked to refer to the codebook and make a single final decision. The codebook includes operational definitions of each variable in each category. The codebook, derived from Stewart and Furse (1986, pp. 131–145) and Laskey et al. (1989), appears in Appendix B.

Judges and Judge Training
Because of the size of the coding project and time involved in this research endeavor, we used 16 judges. All judges were undergraduate students majoring in advertising and all were female. Each commercial took an average of 7 minutes (excluding commercial running time) to code. Each judge coded an average of 6% (80 spots) of the total ($N = 1,340$) sample. This study required many more judges compared to previously mentioned studies because of the amount of coding involved and limited time restraints of each judge. Since judges were undergraduate students, work assignments varied. Judges were compensated with independent study credit or monetarily. In addition, the number of spots each judge

was assigned was limited to the amount of time they had available. Periodic deadlines throughout each coding period (college semester) were enacted to help control for procrastination as well as coder burnout.

There were four coder training meetings. Judges were trained in groups of three or four and each training session lasted approximately 2 hours. The primary researcher conducted each meeting and spent the first part of the training session discussing the goal of the project and its history, as well as explicitly defining each variable in the codebook. The second part of initial training meeting was spent coding three to four sample commercials as a group. The output from sample commercials coded during training was not used in the final analysis. The coding procedure was meticulously reviewed for each commercial and disagreements were resolved out in an open forum. At the conclusion of the meeting judges were instructed to begin the assignment and contact the lead author in case of any questions or concerns.

Pretesting

Pretests were conducted during the initial coder meeting. The lead author chose to use the initial training forum for pretesting since the group discussion led to possible issues and judges could openly question and reference decisions. For example, the lead author would often question decisions made by the group and ask them to explain why they had made those decisions. Using this approach, the lead author could fully discover possible problematic latent definitions which are typically more involving and more difficult to code as well as immediately address these issues to group members. After the initial training meeting, coders were asked to use their knowledge from the meeting and the codebook to make decisions. The lead author was always available for clarification.

Judge Independence

Because many of the coders knew each other, judge independence was critical. Judges were instructed to work independently and not discuss particular coder decisions with other judges. Prior to participating in the study, judges were asked if they had access to a VCR and television in their home. Independence is the basis for reliability (Kassarjian, 1977; Kolbe & Burnett, 1991), and no judgments in the data set were made with a team dynamic.

Number of Judges Per Spot

Each advertisement was initially judged by two coders. The use of two coders was the most frequent configuration found in the literature (Kolbe & Burnett, 1991) and was a realistic way to establish reliability assessments with such a large sample frame. After all commercials had been examined, agreements and disagreements between the coders for each spot were evaluated to establish individual category agreement estimates. Once estimates were taken (to be discussed later) the primary researcher acted as a third coder by solving disagreements and evaluating the work of the judges.

Statistical Evaluation of Intercoder Reliability

Consistent with the content analysis literature, there is no uniform means for addressing intercoder reliability. The importance of addressing interjudge reliability is central to any robust content analysis (Cohen, 1961; Holsti, 1969; Hughes & Garrett, 1990; Kassarjian, 1977; Kolbe & Burnett, 1991; Perreault & Leigh, 1989; Riffe & Freitag, 1997; Riffe et al., 1998), yet the literature offers no consistent way to evaluate. Since the literature does not point to one ideal measure, the onus is on the researcher to judge the best method based on the available information and level of measurement.

Regardless of method chosen, a proportion of agreement must be determined. To determine this proportion, initial estimates were conducted using Holsti's (1969) formula for agreement:

$$\text{Reliability} = \frac{2M}{N_1 + N_2}$$

M = the number of agreements between coders
N = total number of decisions made by each coder

Although Holsti (1969) was used to assess agreement, content analysis methodological literature consistently states valid inter-coder reliability estimates should include a process to correct for chance agreement between coders (Cohen, 1960; Hughes & Garrett, 1990; Kassarjian, 1980; Krippendorff, 1980; Scott, 1955). Including such a measure adds rigor to quantitative content analysis research (Kang et al., 1993). However, studies of content analysis studies found in marketing literature by Kolbe and Burnett (1991) and Hughes and Garrett (1990), as well as communication literature by Riffe and Freitag (1997), did not find frequent use of such methods. Likewise, even in the rare occasions when a method to adjust for chance is used, an aggressive literature search does not yield a consensus decision of which is best. Kang et al. (1993) reviewed content analyses found in the *Journal of Advertising* from 1981 through 1990 discovering 78% of the articles employed a simple percentage of agreement as a measure of reliability, and only 18% of the articles used a method that adjusts for chance agreement.

Scott's pi (1955), Krippendorff's alpha (1980), and Cohen's kappa (1960) appear as frequently used methods for adjusting for chance agreement among judges. Cohen's kappa (1960) is the most frequently used measure, but all three share a similar evaluative structure (Hughes & Garrett, 1990; Perreault & Leigh, 1989):

$$\frac{\% \text{ observed agreement} - \% \text{ expected agreement}}{1 - \% \text{ expected agreement}}$$

However, they differ based on the calculation of expected agreement. Cohen's kappa (1960) is based on the "expected agreement on the marginal numbers from a matrix of proportions. The proportion of a particular value of a category used by one coder is multiplied by the proportion of use of the value of the other coder. These proportions are then added for all the values of the category to get the expected agreement" (Riffe et al., 1998, p. 132). However, Scott's pi differs by calculating expected agreement by using probability theory and looking at the proportion of times each coder uses particular values (Riffe et al., 1998). Krippendorff's (1980) alpha, also a coefficient, resembles Scott's pi. Furthermore, when nominal variables are used with two coders and a large sample size, pi and alpha are equal (Hughes & Garrett, 1990; Perreault & Leigh, 1989; Riffe et al., 1998).

Although pi, alpha, and kappa all appear in the literature as ways to address chance agreement, all three suffer from the same methodological drawback. All address chance agreement by assuming all choices within categories have equal probability of use by both coders. In other words, when coding categories with nominal data and two coders tend to be asymmetrically distributed or if a priori knowledge of the coding distribution is unknown, true reliability estimates can suffer (Hughes & Garrett, 1990; Perreault & Leigh, 1989; Scott, 1955). Since no a priori distribution for any one category is known for the current study, these methods suggest serious limitations. In conclusion, kappa, pi, and alpha are inappropriate for this analysis.

To remedy this reliability problem, Perreault and Leigh (1989) developed a reliability index which does not depend on marginal frequencies. The authors consider their process of assessing reliability more appropriate for marketing studies. Their method still adjusts for chance agreement and has been accepted as a good way to address reliability with two coders and nominal data (Hughes & Garrett, 1990; Rust, 2001; Rust & Cooil, 1994; Kang et al., 1993). Perreault and Leigh (1989) stated,

> Our approach for estimating the reliability of interjudge data is very different from the approach used by Cohen and approaches used in most other research in this area. One major difference is that we do not contrast observed agreement between judges with some estimate of chance agreement, but rather develop an explicit model of the level of agreement that might be expected given the true (population) level of reliability. (p. 140)

The Perreault and Leigh (1989) reliability index (Ir) follows:

$$Ir = \{[(Fo/N) - (1/k)]\,[k/(k-1)]\} \cdot 5$$

Fo = observed frequency of agreement between judges
N = total number of judgments
k = number of categories

EFFIE Sample Reliability Estimates
Holsti (1969) and Perreault and Leigh (1989) findings for each category were computed as well as an overall average. Out of the 51 measured items, both the Holsti (1969) and Perreault and Leigh (1989) formulas found aggregate overall reliability to be .77. This is close to the acceptable range of .80 (Kassarjian, 1977; Poindexter & McCombs, 2000). Furthermore, Riffe et al.

(1998) stated, "Research usually reports reliability in the .80 to .90 range. Research that is breaking new ground with concepts that are rich in analytical value may go forward with reliability levels somewhat below that range" (p. 131). To increase the rigor and robustness of this research, we report individual reliabilities for each variable in Table 2.

Two main reasons account for low-reliability indices: the miscoding of manifest content and the nature of coding latent variables (both will be discussed further in chapter 5). Manifest content variables scoring the lowest based on the Perreault

TABLE 2. Holsti and Perreault and Leigh reliability indices.

Category	Holsti	Perreault and Leigh Index
Scenic beauty	0.91	0.91
Beautiful characters	0.83	0.81
Ugly characters	0.90	0.90
Graphic displays	0.86	0.85
Substantive supers	0.71	0.65
Surrealistic visuals	0.87	0.86
Visual tagline	0.62	0.49
Visual memory device	0.53	0.24
Memorable rhymes, slogans, or mnemonic devices	0.62	0.50
Usual sound effects	0.81	0.79
Spoken tagline	0.65	0.54
Commercial appeals or selling propositions	0.34	0.54
Commercial format	0.41	0.61
Message typology	0.72	0.67
Message typology subtype	0.38	0.56
Rational or emotional appeal	0.54	0.55
Brand-differentiating message	0.62	0.66
Dominant commercial setting	0.75	0.81
Where is the commercial setting?	0.57	0.72

(continued on next page)

TABLE 2. *(continued)*

Category	Holsti	Perreault and Leigh Index
Presence of music	0.87	0.86
Music artist/song known?	0.81	0.78
Music style	0.55	0.68
Music jingle	0.97	0.97
Commercial tone	0.45	0.65
Direct comparison	0.97	0.97
Indirect comparison	0.69	0.61
Puffery or unsubstantiated claim	0.87	0.86
Character hero	0.95	0.95
Brand hero	0.79	0.76
Principle male character	0.84	0.83
Principle female character	0.86	0.85
Principle child or infant	0.91	0.91
Principle character minority	0.90	0.90
Principle character celebrity	0.96	0.96
Principle character actor playing ordinary person	0.55	0.34
Principle character animal	0.97	0.97
Principle character animated	0.96	0.96
No principle characters	0.86	0.85
Character identified with company	0.93	0.92
Background cast	0.76	0.72
Ethnic minority character in minor role	0.79	0.76
Celebrity in minor role	0.96	0.96
Created or cartoon in minor role	0.93	0.92
Real people in minor role	0.91	0.90
Recognized continuing character	0.93	0.93
Presenter/spokesperson on camera	0.85	0.84
Overall reliability average	0.77	0.77

and Leigh reliability index included: visual memory device (.24), principle character actor playing ordinary person (.34), visual tagline (.49), memorable rhymes, slogans, or mnemonic device (.49), and spoken tagline (.54). These low reliabilities are products of systematic coding problems discovered by the primary researcher while in the process of settling disagreements.

The confusion stemmed from the use of the term *tagline* in the operational definition and the use of tagline as taught in advertising practice and curriculum. Wells et al. (2006) stated taglines are, "clever phrases used at the end of an advertisement to summarize the ad's message" (p. 569). Arens (2004) stated taglines (or slogans) are, "A standard company statement for advertisements, salespeople, and company employees. Slogans have two basic purposes: to provide continuity for a campaign and to reduce a key theme or idea to a brief, memorable positioning statement" (p. IT19). These typical definitions of tagline differ from the one first operationalized by Stewart and Furse (1986) and used in our codebook, "A visually presented statement of *new* information at the end of the commercial; for example, the screen shows the name of participating dealers or another product that was not the focus of the commercial shown. Corporate logos or slogans do not qualify." This term confusion was discovered with both visual and audio manifest content and coder reliabilities suffered. In addition, coders were confused regarding the operationalization of actors playing the role of ordinary people and discrepancies were corrected when appropriate by the authors. In sum, these manifest variables were recoded based on the presence or absence of the variable as operationalized by the codebook. For all other categories, the authors solved disagreements by first reviewing the choices of the coders and then assigning the decision. This process is consistent with other content analysis studies using the television commercial as the unit of analysis (Alexander et al., 1998; Browne, 1998; Frazer et al., 2002; Kelley & Turley, 2004).

BUILDING THE FINAL EFFIE SAMPLE

Table 3 lists the 670 EFFIE winners. Silver and bronze awards were not presented until 1999. As a result, this study analyzed

TABLE 3. Total EFFIE sample frequency by award category and year (N = 670).

	2004	2003	2002	2001	2000	1999	1998	1997	1996	1995
Gold	30	25	28	22	28	24	39	30	36	31
Silver	36	32	32	46	33	29	—	—	—	—
Bronze	37	24	24	29	30	25	—	—	—	—

only EFFIE winners from 1999 through 2004 ($n = 534$). We based the rationale for analyzing these years only upon comparability of years and number of EFFIE-award winners available for analysis.

It did not seem logical to include and compare years which had only gold winners to years which had silver and bronze winners. Differences among the awards could limit the comparability of data. To avoid this problem, comparing only gold winners across all years was considered as a solution. However, deleting silver and bronze winners severely reduced (from 534 to 293) the number of commercials to be analyzed. As a result, to keep the sample size robust and allow comparability across years, by including all gold, silver, and bronze winners, only years 1999 through 2004 ($N = 534$) were analyzed.

We made a second methodological adjustment to remedy sample situations violating minimum cell criteria needed for analysis. To address this problem, standard error for the sample was used as a guideline. Standard error for 1999 through 2004 ($N = 534$) was found to be ±4.2% ($n = 22$). To stay within a 95% confidence level, the decision was made to err on the conservative side with an overall rate of ±5% ($n = 27$). In other words, any variable not present in at least 5% of the ads will be excluded from further analysis. Further, special care was taken when examining the results of χ^2 tests for situations in which the

TABLE 4. Total EFFIE spot time by year (N = 534).

(N = 534)	2004	2003	2002	2001	2000	1999	Total
:30	91	66	72	70	78	70	447
:60	11	15	9	20	13	7	75
:15	1	0	3	7	0	1	12

Note. χ^2 (10, n = 534) = 25.595, p = .004.

number of cells with minimum expected cell sizes was greater than desired.

The initial descriptive statistics revealed that the number of 15-second spots (n = 12) violated this five percent threshold. In addition, their presence caused a statistically significant difference (χ^2 (10, N = 534) = 25.595, p = .004) when examining the distribution across years. Specifically, this difference was found to be concentrated in year 2001 (n = 7). As a result, all 15-second spots were eliminated from further analysis.

These deletions reduced the final number of EFFIE awards used for this analysis to 522 total commercials. Table 4 displays total EFFIE spot time by year.

Product Category Decisions
While the proper assignment of product categories is essential to this research, the names of the product categories used by the EFFIE competition have been inconsistent. To remedy this problem, product categories were reassigned based the classification system used by Mediamark Research Inc.'s "Two Year Custom Cable Codebook (2004–2006)." We chose Mediamark (MRI) classifications (Table 5) since advertising practitioners use their data heavily, and detailed descriptions of each product belonging to one of the 25 categories posted in the codebook were readily

TABLE 5. Mediamark Research Inc. product categories with EFFIE examples.

MRI Category	Brand Examples
Apparel/Accessories	Lee Dungarees, Ray-Ban, Converse, Timex
Automotive	Hummer, Nissan, Uniroyal, Toyota
Automotive Aftermarket	Mobil One Oil, Valvoline, Chevron
Beverages	Bud Light, Pepsi Twist, Guinness, Gatorade
Candy/Sweets/Snacks	Hershey's Chocolate, M&Ms, Snickers, Toblar
MRI Category	Brand Examples
Electronics	Canon, Apple, Sprint, Energizer, Nintendo, Sprint
Financial	Citibank, Mastercard, LaSalle Bank, Chase, Invesco
Health and Beauty Aids	Axe, Dove, Neosporin, NyQuil, Zyrtec, Gillette
Home	Maytag, Pella, John Deere, Snakelight, Serta
Household Products—Baby/Children	Crayola, Leap Frog, Gundam, Fisher Price, Lego
Household Products—Food	Cheerios, Dole, Heinz, Kraft, Quaker, Tyson
Household Products—Nonfood	Gain, Rid-X, Cascade, Febreze, Clean Shower
Household Products—Pets	Iams, Tidy Cat, Purina, Frontline, Program
Insurance	CIGNA, Blue Cross Blue Shield
Leisure/Sports	Miami Dolphins, HBO Video, Burger King, Taco Bell
Media	Court TV
MRI Category	Brand Examples
Personal Items	Sharpie, Manco Duck Brand, Hallmark
Shopping	eBay, Wal-Mart, Staples, 7-Eleven, Circuit City
Travel	Delta, Holiday Inn, Norwegian Cruiseline, Harrah's
Trucks/ATV/Motorcycles	Harley Davidson
Internet Products	Monster, MSN, Carfax, Yahoo!
Business Products	UPS, Accenture, Choice Point
PSA/Nonprofit/Government	Georgia Power, U.S. Marines, Big Brothers, Rock the Vote

available. Additional category accommodations were made for public service announcements/government/nonprofit commercials, Internet product ads, and business product ads, since MRI did not provide product categories. Table 5 also provides the names of example brands occupying these categories.

FCB Categories

H1 and H2 theoretically test the thinking and feeling dimensions of the FCB grid proposed by Vaughn (1980). To test these hypotheses, we assigned codes to products appearing both in the EFFIE sample as well as the thinking and feeling dimensions of the FCB grid. Product categories falling on the line between the thinking and feeling dimensions of the FCB grid (see Ratchford, 1987) were excluded.

Data Analysis

SPSS 11.5 and Microsoft Excel were used for data analysis. Frequencies, cross-tabulations, differences in proportions, and chi-square tests were conducted to address the study's research objectives.

CHAPTER 4

RESULTS

This chapter reports the descriptive statistics for the EFFIE sample and the statistical tests of the research objectives. Only categories and variables with significant sample size ($n = 26$) will be statistically tested, and situations in which results were affected by small cell sizes will be identified.

DESCRIPTIVE STATISTICS OF EFFIE COMMERCIALS

Table 6 illustrates EFFIE-award level and award count by year. The year 2004 represented the most awards (19.5%), and 1999 had the fewest (14.5%). Silver (39.1%) was the most frequent award given. No statistically significant differences appeared across years.

TABLE 6. Award year and spot total ($N = 522$).

	1999	2000	2001	2002	2003	2004	Spot Total
Gold	24	28	21	28	25	29	155
	(4.6%)	(5.4%)	(4%)	(5.4%)	(4.8%)	(5.6%)	(29.7%)
Silver	28	33	44	31	32	36	204
	(5.4%)	(6.3%)	(8.4%)	(5.9%)	(6.1%)	(6.9%)	(39.1%)
Bronze	25	30	25	22	24	37	163
	(4.8%)	(5.7%)	(4.8%)	(4.2%)	(4.6%)	(7.1%)	(31.2%)
	77	91	90	81	81	102	522
Total	(14.8%)	(17.4%)	(17.2%)	(15.5%)	(15.5%)	(19.5%)	(100%)

TABLE 7. Spot time by year.

	1999	2000	2001	2002	2003	2004	Year Total
:30	70	78	70	72	66	91	447
	(13.4%)	(14.9%)	(13.4%)	(13.8%)	(12.6%)	(17.4%)	(85.6%)
:60	7	13	20	9	15	11	75
	(1.34%)	(2.5%)	(3.83%)	(1.72%)	(2.87%)	(2.1%)	(14.4%)
	77	91	90	81	81	102	522
Total	(14.8%)	(17.4%)	(17.2%)	(15.5%)	(15.5%)	(19.5%)	(100%)

Spot Time Descriptive Characteristics by Year

The majority of commercials lasted 30 seconds (85.6%) (Table 7). The remaining spots lasted 60 seconds (14.4%). Examining individual years, 2004 contained the most 30-second spots while 2003 contained the most 60-second commercials. However, we discovered no statistically significant differences comparing spot length across years.

MRI Product Category Descriptive Characteristics

Most of the EFFIEs fell into the electronics (10.7%), household products—food (10.7%), health and beauty aids (10.5%), and leisure/sports (10%) categories (Table 8). These four categories accounted for over 40% of the ads. The next most frequent categories included beverages (8%), financial products (7.5%), automotive (6.5%), PSA/nonprofit/government (6.3%), and travel (5.2%). Adding these to the top four categories accounted for over 75% of the EFFIEs. We discovered no statistically significant differences across years and categories. According to the minimum 5% observation rule, all categories less than 5%—from Shopping to Trucks/ATV/Motorcycles—were deleted from further analysis.

TABLE 8. MRI product category distribution.

	Frequency	Percent
Electronics	56	10.7
Health and Beauty Aids	56	10.7
Household Products-Food	55	10.5
Leisure/Sports	52	10.0
Beverages	42	8.0
Financial	39	7.5
Automotive	34	6.5
PSA-Nonprofit-Government	33	6.3
Travel	27	5.2
Shopping	25	4.8
Home	23	4.4
Apparel/Accessories	11	2.1
Household Products—Baby/Children	11	2.1
Household Products—Nonfood	11	2.1
Internet Services	11	2.1
Business Products	11	2.1
Household Products—Pets	7	1.3
Personal Items	5	1.0
Candy/Sweets/Snacks	3	0.6
Insurance	3	0.6
Media	3	0.6
Automotive Aftermarket	2	0.4
Media-Newspaper	1	0.2
Trucks/ATV/Motorcycles	1	0.2
Total	522	100.0

Advertising Agency Brand Descriptive Characteristics

Over 200 total advertising agencies received EFFIE awards from 1999 through 2004. Regional offices of larger agency brands earned many of the awards. In the interest of brevity, we created the descriptive total here by condensing regional offices under a main agency brand name when applicable (e.g., we reclassified FCB NY simply as FCB). This led to 109 advertising agency brands (Table 9). No single agency brand represented more than 6.9% of the total sample, and 143 brands (27.4%) were in less than one percent of the EFFIE sample. Offices of Young & Rubicam

TABLE 9. Advertising agency brand.

	Frequency	Percent
Young & Rubicam	36	6.9
McCann-Erickson	34	6.5
DDB	33	6.3
BBDO	32	6.1
Leo Burnett	29	5.6
FCB	25	4.8
Arnold Worldwide	23	4.4
J. Walter Thompson	23	4.4
Fallon	22	4.2
TBWA Chiat Day	22	4.2
Saatchi & Saatchi	20	3.8
Ogilvy & Mather	15	2.9
Carmicahel Lynch Inc.	11	2.1
Bates USA	8	1.5
Goodby Silverstein & Partners	8	1.5
Grey Advertising	8	1.5
Lowe	8	1.5
D'Arcy	7	1.3
Element 79 Partners LLC	5	1.0
Suissa Miller Advertising	5	1.0
The Martin Agency	5	1.0
Other Agencies (87)	143	27.4
Total	522	100.0

(6.9%) and McCann-Erickson (6.5%) earned the most awards. Other agency offices represented in at least 5% of the total sample include DDB (6.3%), BBDO (6.1%), and Leo Burnett (5.6%).

PREDICTIONS

Prediction 1: *Advertisements for product categories on the FCB grid as thinking products will exhibit more informational message strategies than transformational message strategies.*

Prediction 2: *Advertisements for products categorized on the FCB grid as feeling products will exhibit more transformational message strategies than informational message strategies.*

Findings supported both predictions (Table 10). However, the overall association was weak (χ^2 (1, $n = 96$) = 7.491, $p = .007$); Cramér's $V = .279$, $p = .06$).

Because of this weak association, we conducted a further analysis to examine this relationship by year. The relationship between informational/transformational categories and FCB thinking/feeling dimensions was found statistically significant only in 2003 (χ^2 (1, $n = 14$) = 14, $p = .01$) and marginally significant in 2002 (χ^2 (1, $n = 14$) 4.38, $p = .06$). Once these 2 years were removed, the overall relationship was no longer statistically

TABLE 10. Overall FCB versus message typology.

($n = 96$)	Informational	Transformational	Total
FCB Think	13 (50%)	15 (21.4%)	28 (29.2%)
FCB Feel	13 (50%)	55 (78.6%)	68 (70.8%)
Total	26 (27.1%)	70 (72.9%)	96 (100%)

Note. χ^2 (1, $n = 96$) 7.491, $p = .007$. Cramér's $V = .279$.

TABLE 11. Year 2002 FCB versus message typology.

	Informational	Transformational	Total
FCB Think	4 (80%)	2 (22.2%)	6 (42.9%)
FCB Feel	1 (20%)	7 (77.8%)	8 (57.1%)
Total	5 (35.7%)	9 (64.3%)	14 (100%)

Note. χ^2 (1, n = 90) = 4.38, p = .06.

TABLE 12. Year 2003 FCB versus message typology.

	Informational	Transformational	Total
FCB Think	2 (100%)	0 (0%)	2 (14.3%)
FCB Feel	0 (0%)	12 (100%)	12 (85.7%)
Total	2 (14.3%)	12 (85.7%)	14 (100%)

Note. χ^2 (1, n = 90) = 14, p = .01.

significant. Table 11 and Table 12 display years 2002 and 2003, respectively.

RESEARCH QUESTIONS

Research Question 1: *What trends have occurred over time regarding informational and transformational message strategies found in EFFIE-award-winning campaigns?*

This research question investigated the use of informational and transformational message strategies and their respective subtypes.

We found a statistically significant difference (χ^2 (5, n = 522) = 42.102, p < .001) when comparing years to the use of informational and transformational messages (Table 13). More than expected informational message strategies appeared in

2000. In addition, transformational strategies appeared more than expected in 2003 and 2004.

The second part of this research question investigated the use of message subtype by year. Because of sample-size criteria, we probed only user image, brand image, USP, use occasion, and preemptive. Table 14 displays the frequencies and percentages of each subcategory in the total EFFIE sample.

TABLE **13.** Overall use of message strategy by year.

Year	1999 (%)	2000 (%)	2001 (%)	2002 (%)	2003 (%)	2004 (%)	Total
Informational	26 (33.7)	43 (8.2)	27 (30)	24 (29.6)	9 (11.1)	13 (12.7)	142 (27.2)
Transformational	51 (66.2)	48 (52.7)	63 (70)	57 (70.3)	72 (88.9)	89 (87.2)	380 (72.8)
Total (% of total)	77 (14.6)	91 (17.4)	90 (17.2)	81 (15.5)	81 (15.5)	102 (19.5)	522 (100)

Note. χ^2 (5, n = 522) = 42.102, p < .001. Cramér's V = .284.

TABLE **14.** Distribution of message subtype.

Message Subtype	Frequency	Percent
User Image	156	29.9
Brand Image	152	29.1
USP	69	13.2
Use Occasion	63	12.1
Preemptive	55	10.5
Comparative	11	2.1
Generic Transformational	5	1.0
Generic Informational	4	0.8
Hyperbole	3	0.6
Informational Other	2	0.4
Transformational Other	2	0.4
Total	522	100

The examined message subcategories exhibited overall statistically significant differences in groups (χ^2 (20, $n = 495$) = 62.147, $p < .001$). Results indicate higher than expected uses of informational subcategories such as USP in 1999 and 2000 and preemptive in 2000. Consistent with the overall relationship illustrated in Table 13, transformational categories such as brand image in 2003 and use occasion in 2004 appeared in the sample more than expected. Table 15 presents the cross-tabulation of message typology subcategories by year.

Research Question 2: *Do certain product categories have consistent message typologies over time?*

We analyzed sample size for each product category to determine which MRI categories exceeded the 5% sample-size-inclusion criteria and found 8 product categories met the sample

TABLE **15.** Message typology subcategories by year.

	1999 (%)	2000 (%)	2001 (%)	2002 (%)	2003 (%)	2004 (%)	Total (%)
User Image	22	27	28	25	23	31	156
	(29.3)	(31.8)	(33.7)	(31.3)	(30.7)	(32)	(31.5)
Brand Image	25	13	24	25	33	32	152
	(33.3)	(15.3)	(28.9)	(31.3)	(44)	(33)	(30.7)
USP	17	23	9	11	3	6	69
	(22.7)	(27.1)	(10.8)	(13.8)	(4)	(6.2)	(13.9)
Use Occasion	3	7	11	7	13	22	63
	(4)	(8.2)	(13.3)	(8.8)	(17.3)	(22.7)	(12.7)
Preemptive	8	15	11	12	3	6	55
	(10.7)	(17.6)	(13.3)	(15)	(4)	(6.2)	(11.1)
	75	85	83	80	75	97	495
Total	(15.2)	(17.2)	(16.8)	(16.2)	(15.2)	(19.6)	(100)

Note. χ^2 (20, $n = 495$) = 62.147, $p < .001$. Cramér's $V = .177$.

criteria. Chi-square analysis comparing product categories to message types by year yielded two statistically significant associations: automotive (χ^2 (5, $n = 34$) = 15.59, $p = .008$) and travel (χ^2 (5, $n = 27$) = 11.56, $p = .04$). Table 16 provides a list of included MRI categories with frequency and percentage of presence as well as statistical significance.

TABLE 16. MRI categories exceeding 5% threshold.

	Frequency	Percent	Typology by Year		
			χ^2	df	p value
Electronics	56	10.7	9.65	5	0.09
Health and Beauty Aids	56	10.7	4.08	5	0.54
Household Products—Food	55	10.5	1.76	5	0.06
Leisure/Sports	52	10.0	6.31	5	0.278
Beverages	42	8.0	8.01	5	0.16
Financial	39	7.5	4.69	5	0.46
Automotive	34	6.5	15.59	5	.008*
PSA-Nonprofit-Government	33	6.3	4.16	5	0.526
Travel	27	5.2	11.55	5	0.04*
Total	394	75.5			

*$p < .05$.

TABLE 17. Automotive product category message typology by year.

Year	1999 (%)	2000 (%)	2001 (%)	2002 (%)	2003 (%)	2004 (%)	Total
Informational	0	5	0	1	0	0	6
	(0)	(62.5)	(0)	(20)	(0)	(0)	(17.6)
Transformational	4	3	7	4	5	5	28
	(100)	(37.5)	(100)	(80)	(100)	(100)	(82.4)
Total	4	7	5	5	5	5	34
(%)	(11.8)	(20.6)	(14.7)	(14.7)	(14.7)	(14.7)	(100)

Note. χ^2 (5, $n = 34$) = 15.59, $p = .008$. Cramér's $V = .677$.

The automotive and travel MRI product category both display dependent relationship associations when comparing message typology used by year. Furthermore, both tend to use more transformational messages than informational. The strength of the association was strongest for automotive (Cramér's V = .677) but also strong for travel (Cramér's V = .654). Both MRI product categories favor the use of transformational message typologies.

Research Question 3: *What are the significant differences in executional characteristics between informational and transformational EFFIE television advertisements?*

Measured executional devices individually addressed included: visual devices, auditory devices, commercial appeals or selling propositions, commercial structures, commercial format, commercial approach, commercial setting, music, tone, indirect comparisons, and characters. Because of sample criteria restraints, only the overall informational and transformational strategies were investigated. In addition, variables were excluded if they did not meet the 5% sample inclusion criteria.

TABLE 18. Travel product category message typology by year.

Year	1999 (%)	2000 (%)	2001 (%)	2002 (%)	2003 (%)	2004 (%)	Total (%)
Informational	0	0	3	1	0	0	4
	(0)	(0)	(60)	(25)	(0)	(0)	(14.8)
Transformational	5	4	2	3	5	4	23
	(100)	(100)	(40)	(75)	(100)	(100)	(85.2)
Total	5	4	90	81	5	4	27
(% of total)	(18.5)	(14.8)	(17.2)	(15.5)	(18.5)	(14.8)	(100)

Note. χ^2 (5, n = 27) = 11.56, p = .04. Cramér's V = .654.

Table 19 displays frequencies, percentages, and dependent relationship significance for all measured visual devices. Visual memory devices (99.4%) were the most common visual device found in the overall EFFIE sample. However, only substantive supers had a dependent statistical relationship (χ^2 (1, n = 522) = 3.47, p = .039) with a more than expected presence in informational commercials (Table 20).

Memorable rhymes, slogans, or mnemonic devices (79%) appeared as the most common auditory device in the overall sample as well as the only auditory device exhibiting a relationship with message strategy (Table 21). Almost 87% (86.6%) of

TABLE 19. Presence of visual devices in message typology.

	Frequency	Percent	Typology Significance
Visual Memory Device	519	99.4	0.385
Substantive Supers	274	52.5	0.039*
Surrealistic Visuals	93	17.8	0.375
Beautiful Characters	73	14	0.057
Visual Tagline	65	12.5	0.078
Scenic Beauty	59	11.3	0.216
Graphic Display	21	4	ns**
Ugly Characters	13	2.5	ns**

*p < .05. **Sample size criteria violation (N = 522).

TABLE 20. Substantive supers in message typology.

	Informational (%)	Transformational (%)	Total (%)
Presence	84 (59.2)	190 (50)	274 (52.5)
Absence	58 (40.8)	190 (50)	248 (47.5)
Total (%)	142 (27.2)	380 (72.8)	522.0

Note. χ^2 (1, n = 522) = 3.47, p = .039. Cramér's V = .082.

TABLE 21. Auditory devices present in overall sample.

(N = 522)	Frequency	Percent	Typology Significance
Memorable Rhymes, Slogans, or Mnemonic Devices	408	79	0.002*
Spoken Tagline	56	10.7	0.338
Unusual Sound Effects	20	3.8	ns

TABLE 22. Memorable rhymes, slogans or mnemonic devices, and message typology.

Memorable Rhymes, Slogans, or Mnemonic	Informational	Transformational	Total (%)
Presence	123 (86.6)	285 (75)	408 (78.2)
Absence	19 (13.4)	95 (25)	114 (21.8)
Total (%)	142 (27.2)	380 (72.8)	522.0

Note. χ^2 (1, n = 522) = 8.18, p = .002. Cramér's V = .125.

all informational message strategies used a memorable rhyme, slogan, or mnemonic device (χ^2 (1, n = 522) = 8.18, p = .002).

Commercial appeals and selling propositions were measured to investigate if specific appeals gravitated toward specific message strategies. Product performance or benefit as main message (29.9%) appeared as the most common appeal. We excluded seven appeals from analysis because of sample size yielding six total measured appeals (Table 23).

Commercial appeals showed statistically significance related to message strategy (χ^2 (5, n = 446) = 95.42, p < .001) (Table 24). Product performance or benefit presented in almost two-thirds (63.8%) of informational message strategies in the truncated sample. Furthermore, product reminder as main message, enjoyment

TABLE **23.** Commercial appeals or selling propositions present in overall sample.

	Frequency	Percent
Product Performance or Benefit as Main Message	156	29.9
Product Reminder as Main Message	90	17.2
Enjoyment Appeals	84	12.5
Psychological or Subjective Benefits as Main Message	52	10.0
Attribute or Ingredients as Main Message	50	9.6
Excitement, Sensation, Variety	35	6.7
Achievement*	23	4.4
Safety Appeals*	20	3.1
Welfare Appeals*	16	3.0
Self-esteem or Self-image*	11	2.1
Sexual Appeals*	5	1.0
Comfort Appeals*	5	1.0
Social Approval*	0	0.0

*Sample size criteria violation (N = 522).

appeals as well as excitement, sensation, and variety appeals were all related to transformational message strategies.

Blind lead-in (29.3%) and front-end impact (28.5%) commercial structures were the most commonly found structures (Table 25). Three commercial structure styles were in less than 5% of the total sample and were removed from analysis.

The relationship between overall commercial structure and message typology was significant (χ^2 (4, n = 477) = 36.07, $p < .001$) (Table 26). Commercial structures found in commercials with an informational message strategy include front-end impact and message in the middle. Blind lead-in and humorous closing appeared significantly more often than expected in transformational message strategies.

TABLE 24. Commercial appeals or selling propositions and message typology.

	Informational (%)	Transformational (%)	Total (%)
Attribute/Ingredients as Main Message	23 (46)	27 (54)	50 (11.2)
Product Performance or Benefit as Main Message	83 (53.2)	73 (46.8)	156 (35)
Psychological or Subjective Benefits as Main Message	7 (13.5)	45 (86.5)	52 (11.7)
Product Reminder as Main Message	11 (12.2)	79 (87.8)	90 (20.2)
Enjoyment Appeals	6 (9.5)	57 (90.5)	63 (14.1)
Excitement, Sensation, Variety	0 (0)	35 (100)	35 (7.8)
Total (%)	130 (29.1)	316 (70.9)	446 (100)

Note. χ^2 (5, n = 446) = 95.42, p < .001. Cramér's V = .463.

TABLE 25. Commercial structures present in overall sample.

	Frequency	Percent
Blind Lead-in	153	29.3
Front-end Impact	149	28.5
Humorous Closing	121	23.2
Message in the Middle	54	10.3
Unusual Setting or Situation*	21	4.0
Surprise or Suspense at Closing*	16	3.1
Surprise or Suspense in the Middle*	8	1.5

*Sample size criteria violation (N = 522).

We measured a total of 18 commercial formats. Descriptively, comedy or satire (25.1%) represented the most common format while photographic stills (.2%) was the least common (Table 27). Of the original 18, we eliminated 10 because of sample-size criteria reducing final measurement to 8 formats.

TABLE 26. Commercial structure by message typology.

	Informational (%)	Transformational (%)	Total (%)
Blind Lead-in	28 (18.3)	125 (81.7)	153 (32.1)
Front-end Impact	61 (40.9)	88 (59.1)	149 (29.9)
Humorous Closing	19 (15.7)	102 (84.3)	121 (32.2)
Message in the Middle	24 (44.4)	30 (55.6)	54 (11.3)
Total (%)	132 (27.7)	345 (72.3)	477 (100)

Note. χ^2 (4, n = 477) = 36.07, p < .001. Cramér's V = .275.

TABLE 27. Commercial format present in overall sample.

(*N* = 522)	Frequency	Percent
Comedy or Satire	131	25.1
Creation of Mood or Image as Dominant Element	74	14.2
Demonstration of Product in Use or by Analogy	46	8.8
Slice of Life	43	8.2
Continuity of Action	40	7.7
Vignette	32	6.1
Testimonial by Product User	32	6.1
Fantasy, Exaggeration or Surrealism as Dominant Element	28	5.4
Endorsement of Celebrity or Authority*	22	4.2
Demonstration of Results of Using Product*	19	3.6
Announcement*	17	3.3
Animation/Cartoon/Rotoscope*	15	2.9
Problem and Solution (Before/After Presentation)*	11	2.1
New Wave (Product Graphics)*	4	0.8
Camera Involves Audience in Situation*	3	0.6
Commercial Written as Serious Drama*	2	0.4
Interview (Person on the Street or Elsewhere)*	2	0.4
Photographic Stills*	1	0.2

*Sample size criteria violation (*N* = 522).

Cross-tabulation discovered an overall significant relationship between commercial format and message typology (χ^2 (7, n = 426) = 28.18, p < .001) with three formats deviating from independence. Testimonial by product user and demonstration of product in use or by analogy occurred more than expected in informational message strategies, while the creation of a mood or image as dominant element related to transformational message typologies.

Stewart and Furse (1996) used commercial approach to operationalize in three dimensions the rational and emotional characteristics manifested in television commercials: more rational, balance of rational and emotional, and more emotional. This differs from the dichotomous Laskey et al. (1989) characteristic classifications. When comparing Stewart and Furse's commercial approach to Laskey et al.'s message typologies using the

TABLE 28. Commercial format and message typology.

	Informational (%)	Transformational (%)	Total (%)
Comedy or Satire	24 (18.3)	107 (81.7)	131 (30.8)
Creation of Mood or Image as Dominant Element	8 (10.8)	66 (81.7)	74 (17.4)
Demonstration of Product in Use or by Analogy	20 (43.5)	26 (56.5)	46 (10.8)
Slice of Life	10 (23.3)	33 (76.7)	43 (10.1)
Continuity of Action	13 (32.5)	27 (67.5)	40 (9.4)
Vignette	6 (18.8)	26 (81.3)	32 (7.5)
Testimonial by Product User	14 (43.8)	18 (56.3)	32 (7.5)
Fantasy, Exaggeration, or Surrealism as Dominant Element	6 (21.4)	22 (78.6)	28 (6.5)
Total (%)	101 (23.7)	325 (76.3)	426 (100)

Note. χ^2 (7, n = 426) = 28.18, p < .001. Cramér's V = .257.

EFFIE sample, dependence was discovered (χ^2 (2, n = 522) = 223.25, p < .05) (Table 29). Informational typologies emerged in over 97% of the more rational approaches, while over 99% of the more emotional approaches exhibited transformational typology characteristics. However, commercials exhibiting a balance of rational and emotional showed more informational characteristics.

Cross-tabulations comparing the relationship between brand-differentiating messages and message typology showed a statistically significant relationship (χ^2 (1, n = 522) = 89.3, p < .001) (Table 30). Results indicate informational ads exhibited the presence of brand-differentiating characteristics more than when compared to transformational messages.

TABLE 29. Commercial approach and message typology.

	Informational	Transformational	Total
More Rational (%)	41 (97.6)	1 (2.4)	42 (8)
Balance of Rational and Emotional (%)	99 (43.2)	130 (56.8)	229 (42.9)
More Emotional (%)	2 (.8)	249 (99.2)	251 (48.1)
Total (%)	142 (27.2)	380 (72.8)	522

Note. χ^2 (2, n = 522) = 223.25, p < .05. Cramér's V = .654.

TABLE 30. Brand-differentiating message and message typology.

	Informational	Transformational	Total (%)
Presence (%)	103 (50)	103 (50)	206 (39.5)
Absence (%)	39 (12.3)	277 (87.7)	316 (60.5)
Total (%)	142 (27.2)	380 (72.8)	522 (100)

Note. χ^2 (1, n = 522) = 89.3, p < .001. Cramér's V = .414.

We measured commercial setting by evaluating the dominant locale as: indoors, outdoors, other, or no setting (Table 31). The relationship between the dominant commercial setting and message typology demonstrated dependence (χ^2 (3, n = 463) = 8.04, p = .05). Situations with no setting tended to have more informational message strategies than expected. Conversely, outdoor settings tend to exhibit more transformational strategies.

We measured the use of music by examining: the presence of music, music as a major element, music in commercial recognizable (known song or artist), and the presence of a brand jingle (Table 32). The presence of music as a major element was

TABLE 31. Dominant commercial setting and message typology.

	Informational	Transformational	Total (%)
Indoors (%)	65 (28.9)	160 (71.1)	225 (43.1)
Outdoors (%)	35 (21.1)	131 (78.9)	166 (31.8)
Other (%)	21 (26.6)	58 (73.4)	79 (15.1)
None (%)	21 (40.4)	31 (59.6)	52 (10)
Total (%)	142 (27.2)	380 (72.8)	522

Note. χ^2 (3, n = 463) = 8.04, p = .05. Cramér's V = .124.

TABLE 32. Presence of music devices in overall sample.

(N = 522)	Frequency	Percent	p
Presence of Music in Commercials	433	83	0.431
Presence of Music as a Major Element	86	16.5	0.016*
Music Artist or Song Recognizable	50	9.6	0.264
Brand Jingle Present**	23	4.4	*ns*

*p < .05. **Sample size criteria violation (N = 522).

the only significant relationship (χ^2 (1, n = 522) = 4.95, p = .02) with message typology.

Music as a major element was found more than expected in commercials exhibiting transformational message strategies (Table 33).

TABLE 33. Music as a major element and message typology.

	Informational	Transformational	Total
Presence (%)	15 (17.4)	71 (82.6)	86 (16.5)
Absence (%)	127 (29.1)	309 (70.9)	436 (83.5)
Total (%)	142 (27.2)	380 (72.8)	522 (100)

Note. χ^2 (1, n = 522) = 4.95, p = .02. Cramér's V = .097.

TABLE 34. Presence of commercial tone and atmosphere in overall sample.

(N = 522)	Frequency	Percent
Humorous	212	40.6
Happy/Fun-loving	57	10.9
Warm and Caring	40	7.7
Somber/Serious	34	6.5
Cute/Adorable*	23	4.4
Suspenseful*	23	4.4
Technological/Futuristic*	22	4.2
Wholesome/Healthy*	18	3.4
Cool/Laid Back*	15	2.9
Relaxed/Comfortable*	13	2.5
Rough/Rugged*	13	2.5
Hard Sell*	12	2.3
Modern/Contemporary*	11	2.1
Glamorous*	11	2.1
Old Fashioned/Nostalgic*	8	1.5
Conservative/Traditional*	6	1.1
Uneasy/Tense/Irritated*	4	0.8

*Sample size criteria violation (N = 522).

Over 40% of the entire sample exhibited a humorous tone or atmosphere (Table 34). However, only 4 of 17 categories of commercial tone and atmosphere met the 5% minimum observation rule. However, upon comparison of the four, no statistically significant differences appeared.

The use of comparative advertising and puffery was examined within message typology. The presence of direct comparisons and puffery were not present in at least 5% of the EFFIE sample, so both were excluded from statistical analysis. Indirect comparisons (χ^2 (1, $n = 522$) = 70.96, $p < .001$) yielded a statistically significant dependence relationship (Table 36).

Indirect comparisons (Table 37) were present in over 34% of sample and tended to be present more than expected with informational message typologies.

TABLE 35. Comparisons and puffery use in overall sample.

	Frequency	Percent
Direct Comparison	17	3.3
Indirect Comparison*	181	65.3
Puffery or Unsubstantiated Claim**	16	3.1

*$p < .05$. **Sample size criteria violation ($N = 522$).

TABLE 36. Indirect comparisons and message typology.

	Informational	Transformational	Total (%)
Presence (%)	90 (49.7)	91 (50.3)	181 (34.7)
Absence (%)	52 (15.2)	289 (84.8)	341 (65.3)
Total (%)	142 (27.2)	380 (72.8)	522 (100)

Note. χ^2 (1, $n = 522$) = 70.96, $p < .001$. Cramér's $V = .369$.

TABLE 37. Commercial characters present in overall sample.

	Frequency	Percent
Principle Character Male*	326	62.5
Principle Character Actor Playing Role of Ordinary Person	299	57.3
Background Cast*	299	57.3
Principle Character Female	191	36.6
Racial or Ethnic Minority Character in Minor Role*	132	25.3
Principle Character Child or Infant	91	17.4
Presenter/Spokesperson on Camera*	84	16.1
Principle Character Racial or Ethnic Minority*	81	15.5
No Principle Character(s)	75	14.4
Principle Character Celebrity	51	9.8
Character(s) Identified with Company	49	9.4
Recognized Continuing Character	44	8.4
Celebrity in Minor Role (Cameo Appearance)	26	7.9
Animal(s) in Minor Role	41	7.9
Principle Character(s) Creation	40	7.7
Principle Character(s) Animal	31	5.9
Principle Character Real People	30	5.7
Principle Character(s) Animated	27	5.2
Real Person(s) in Minor Role	26	5
Created Character or Cartoon Character in Minor Role**	18	3.4

*$p < .05$. **Sample size criteria violation ($N = 522$).

The final examination for research question three involved the use of commercial characters within message typologies. The presence of 20 character types was measured. Principle male characters (62.5%), along with principle character actor playing the role of ordinary person (57.3), and the use of a background cast (57.3%) appeared most commonly (Table 38). In addition,

TABLE **38.** Presence of commercial characters and message typology.

	Presence						
	Informational	Transformational	Total	χ^2	df	p	Cramér's V
Principle Character Male	79 (24.2)	247 (75.8)	326 (62.5)	3.87	1	0.03	0.086
Background Cast	71 (23.7)	228 (76.3)	299 (57.3)	4.22	1	0.03	0.09
Racial or Ethnic Minority in Minor Role	24 (18.2)	108 (81.8)	132 (25.3)	7.26	1	0.004	0.118
Presenter/Spokesperson on Camera	37 (44)	47 (56)	84 (16.1)	14.34	1	<.001	0.166
Principle Character Racial or Ethnic Minority	11 (13.6)	70 (86.4)	81 (15.5)	8.99	1	0.001	0.131

characters classified as an ethnic minority were present more in a minor (25.3%) role than in a major (15.5%) role.

Five significant associations (Table 39) emerged after comparing the use of characters with message typology: principle male, background cast, use of a presenter or spokesperson on camera, and racial or ethnic minority in minor role and as primary character(s). Principle male characters (χ^2 (1, n = 522) = 3.87, p = .03), background cast (χ^2 (1, n = 522) = 4.22, p = .03), racial or ethnic minority in a principle (χ^2 (1, n = 522) = 8.99. p = .001) and minor role (χ^2 (1, n = 522) = 7.26, p = .004) all exhibited higher than expected presence in transformational typologies. The presenter/spokesperson on camera (χ^2 (1, n = 522) = 14.34, p < .001) characteristic was present more than expected in informational typologies.

Research Question 4: *What trends have occurred over time regarding executional factors found in EFFIE-award-winning commercials?*

We measured each executional device for association change by year. Executional characteristics demonstrating association change included:

- Beautiful characters
- Commercial appeals/selling propositions
- Commercial approaches
- Commercial formats
- Commercial structures
- Principle character(s) actor in role of ordinary person
- Presenter/spokesperson on camera
- Principle female characters
- Scenic beauty
- Spoken taglines
- Visual taglines

TABLE 39. Use of scenic beauty by year.

	1999	2000	2001	2002	2003	2004	Total (%)
Presence	13	16	10	9	6	5	59
	(16.9)	(17.6)	(11.1)	(11.1)	(7.4)	(4.9)	(11.3)
Absence	64	75	80	72	75	97	463
	(83.1)	(82.4)	(88.9)	(88.9)	(92.6)	(95.1)	(88.7)
	77	91	90	81	81	102	
Total	(14.8)	(17.4)	(17.2)	(15.5)	(15.5)	(19.5)	522.0

Note. χ^2 (5, n = 522) = 11.37, p = .04. Cramér's V = .148.

TABLE 40. Use of beautiful characters by year.

	1999	2000	2001	2002	2003	2004	Total (%)
Presence	10	26	13	11	4	9	73
	(13)	(28.6)	(14.4)	(13.5)	(4.9)	(8.8)	(14)
Absence	67	65	77	70	77	98	449
	(87)	(71.4)	(85.6)	(86.4)	(95)	(91.2)	(86)
	77	91	90	81	81	102	
Total (%)	(14.8)	(17.4)	(17.2)	(15.5)	(15.5)	(19.5)	522

Note. χ^2 (5, n = 522) = 23.96, p < .001. Cramér's V = .214.

Categories such as commercial appeals, commercial structures, and commercial formats were truncated as they were in research question three to meet the minimum sample criteria for analysis.

The use of visual elements scenic beauty ($\chi 2$ (5, n = 522) = 11.37, p = .04), beautiful characters (χ^2 (5, n = 522) = 23.96, p < .001), and visual taglines (χ^2 (5, n = 522) = 37.4, p < .001) exhibited dependence relationships by year. Scenic beauty contained more presence than expected in 1999 and 2000. Beautiful characters appeared more often than expected in 2000 com-

TABLE 41. Use of visual taglines by year.

	1999	2000	2001	2002	2003	2004	Total (%)
Presence	7	17	5	4	4	28	65
	(9.1)	(18.7)	(5.6)	(4.9)	(4.9)	(27.4)	(12.5)
Absence	70	74	85	77	77	74	457
	(91)	(81.3)	(94.4)	(95.1)	(95.1)	(72.5)	(87.55)
	77	91	90	81	81	102	
Total	(14.8)	(17.4)	(17.2)	(15.5)	(15.5)	(19.5)	522

Note. χ^2 (5, n = 522) = 37.4, p < .001. Cramér's V = .268.

TABLE 42. Use of spoken taglines by year.

	1999	2000	2001	2002	2003	2004	Total
Presence	4	10	5	9	6	22	56
	(5.2)	(11)	(5.6)	(11.1)	(7.4)	(21.6)	(10.7)
Absence	73	81	85	72	75	80	466
	(94.8)	(89)	(94.4)	(88.9)	(92.6)	(78.4)	(89.3)
	77	91	90	81	81	102	
Total	(14.8)	(17.4)	(17.2)	(15.5)	(15.5)	(19.5)	522

Note. χ^2 (5, n = 522) = 18.44, p = .002. Cramér's V = .188.

pared to other years. Visual taglines appeared more often than expected in 2004. Tables 40–42 display distributions for scenic beauty, beautiful characters, and visual taglines respectively.

The use of spoken taglines (χ^2 (5, n = 522) = 18.44, p = .002) represented the only significant auditory device finding when comparing across years. The year 2004 contained more presence than expected (Table 43).

Commercial appeals or selling propositions (χ^2 (25, n = 446) = 45.29, p = .008) exhibited change over time within different variables (Table 44). Product performance or benefit as main

TABLE 43. Commercial appeals or selling propositions by year.

	1999	2000	2001	2002	2003	2004	Total
Product Performance or Benefit as Main Message	26 (36.6)	33 (42.9)	25 (32.5)	23 (33.3)	21 (30.4)	28 (33.7)	156 (35)
Product Reminder as Main Message	16 (22.5)	11 (14.3)	12 (15.6)	15 (21.7)	13 (18.8)	23 (27.7)	90 (20.2)
Enjoyment Appeals	6 (8.5)	18 (23.4)	8 (10.4)	8 (11.6)	12 (17.4)	11 (13.2)	63 (14.1)
Psychological or Subjective Benefits as Main Message	11 (15.5)	2 (2.6)	18 (23.4)	9 (13)	6 (8.6)	6 (7.2)	52 (11.7)
Attribute or Ingredients as Main Message	8 (11.3)	11 (14.3)	9 (11.7)	8 (11.6)	5 (7.2)	9 (10.8)	50 (11.2)
Excitement, Sensation, Variety	4 (5.6)	2 (2.6)	5 (6.5)	6 (8.7)	12 (17.4)	6 (7.2)	35 (7.8)
Total	71 (16)	77 (17.2)	77 (17.3)	69 (15.5)	69 (15.4)	83 (18.6)	446

Note. χ^2 (25, n = 446) = 45.29, p = .008. Cramér's V = .143.

message and enjoyment appeals ranked higher than expected in 2000. Psychological or subjective benefits as main message appeared less often than expected in 2000 and more often than expected in 2001. Lastly, appeals with the product as a reminder appeared more often than expected in 2004.

Relationships appeared when comparing the use of commercial structures (χ^2 (15, $n = 477$) = 32.79, $p = .005$) across years (Table 45). Blind lead-in structures appeared more than expected in 2002. The year 2004 displayed more than expected front-end impact structures. Humorous closing structures appeared less than expected in 1999. Message-in-the-middle structures were found less often than expected in 2004 while unusual settings and situation structures were found more often than expected in 2004.

Commercial formats changed across years (χ^2 (35, $n = 426$) = 72.98, $p < .001$) (Table 46). Creation of a mood appeared more than expected in 2001 and less than expected in 2004. Slice-of-life formats were found more than expected in 2000. Vignettes

TABLE 44. Use of commercial structures by year.

	1999	2000	2001	2002	2003	2004	Total
Blind Lead-in	24	19	28	33	23	26	153
	(33.8)	(23.5)	(32.9)	(41.8)	(30.3)	(30.6)	(32.1)
Front-end	29	23	20	22	17	38	149
Impact	(40.8)	(28.4)	(23.5)	(27.8)	(22.4)	(44.7)	(31.2)
Humorous	9	25	27	18	25	17	121
Closing	(12.7)	(30.9)	(31.8)	(22.8)	(32.9)	(20)	(25.4)
Message	9	14	10	6	11	4	54
in the Middle	(12.7)	(17.3)	(11.8)	(7.6)	(14.5)	(4.7)	(11.3)
	71	81	85	79	76	85	
Total	(14.9)	(17)	(17.8)	(16.6)	(15.9)	(17.8)	477.0

Note. χ^2 (15, $n = 477$) = 32.79, $p = .005$. Cramér's $V = .151$.

TABLE 45. Use of commercial format by year.

	1999	2000	2001	2002	2003	2004	Total
Comedy or Satire	12 (21.4)	25 (32.5)	27 (35.5)	18 (27.7)	25 (37.3)	24 (28.2)	131 (30.8)
Creation of Mood or Image as Dominant Element	13 (23.2)	12 (15.6)	20 (26.3)	12 (18.5)	11 (16.4)	6 (7.1)	74 (17.4)
Demonstration of Product in Use or by Analogy	5 (8.9)	4 (5.2)	9 (11.8)	8 (12.3)	8 (11.9)	12 (14.1)	46 (10.8)
Slice of Life	5 (8.9)	18 (23.4)	4 (5.3)	5 (7.7)	4 (6)	7 (8.2)	43 (10.1)
Continuity of Action	9 (16.1)	4 (5.2)	4 (5.3)	9 (13.8)	3 (4.5)	11 (12.9)	40 (9.4)
Testimonial by Product User	3 (5.4)	3 (3.9)	5 (6.6)	10 (15.4)	4 (6)	7 (8.2)	32 (7.5)
Vignette	2 (3.6)	7 (9.1)	2 (2.6)	1 (1.5)	6 (9)	14 (16.5)	32 (7.5)
Fantasy, Exaggeration or Surrealism as Dominant Element	7 (12.5)	4 (5.2)	5 (6.6)	2 (3.1)	6 (9)	4 (4.7)	28 (6.6)
Total	56 (13.1)	77 (18.1)	76 (17.8)	65 (15.3)	67 (15.7)	85 (20)	426.0

Note. χ^2 (35, $n = 426$) = 72.98, $p < .001$. Cramér's $V = .185$.

appeared more than expected in 2004 and less than expected in 2002.

The use of commercial approaches (χ^2 (5, n = 522) = 13.75, p = .01) exhibited dependence characteristics when examined by year (Table 47). The presence of a more than expected balance of rational and emotional approaches appeared in 2000 with a less than expected presence of more emotional ads appearing that same year. Also, less than expected presence of more rational commercial approaches occurred in 2004.

TABLE 46. Use of commercial approach by year.

	1999	2000	2001	2002	2003	2004	Total
More Rational	10	11	7	7	4	3	42
	(13)	(12.1)	(7.8)	(8.6)	(4.9)	(2.9)	(8)
Balance of Rational	25	49	40	39	30	46	229
and Emotional	(32.5)	(53.8)	(44.4)	(48.1)	(37)	(45.1)	(43.9)
More Emotional	42	31	43	35	47	53	251
	(54.5)	(34.1)	(47.5)	(43.2)	(58)	(52)	(48.1)
	77	91	90	81	81	102	
Total	(14.8)	(17.4)	(17.2)	(15.5)	(15.5)	(19.5)	522.0

Note. χ^2 (5, n = 522) = 13.75, p = .01. Cramér's V = .162.

TABLE 47. Use of female characters by year.

	1999	2000	2001	2002	2003	2004	Total
Yes	14	37	32	42	37	29	191
	(18.2)	(40.7)	(35.6)	(51.9)	(45.7)	(28.4)	(36.6)
No	63	54	58	39	44	73	331
	(81.8)	(59.3)	(64.4)	(48.1)	(54.3)	(71.6)	(63.4)
	77	91	90	81	81	102	
Total	(14.8)	(17.4)	(17.2)	(15.5)	(15.5)	(19.5)	522.0

Note. χ^2 (5, n = 522) = 25.88, p = .01. Cramér's V = .223.

TABLE **48.** Use of principle character(s) playing role of ordinary person.

	2004	2003	2002	2001	2000	1999	Total
Yes	59	43	53	58	55	31	299
	(57.8)	(53.1)	(65.4)	(64.4)	(60.4)	(40.3)	(57.3)
No	43	38	28	32	36	46	223
	(42.2)	(46.9)	(34.6)	(35.6)	(39.6)	(59.7)	(42.7)
	102	81	81	90	91	77	
Total	(19.5)	(15.5)	(15.5)	(17.2)	(17.4)	(14.8)	522.0

Note. χ^2 (5, n = 522) = 14.17, p = .02. Cramér's V = .015.

TABLE **49.** Use of presenter/spokesperson on camera by year.

	1999	2000	2001	2002	2003	2004	Total
Yes	14	21	7	18	7	17	84
	(18.2)	(23.1)	(7.8)	(22.2)	(8.6)	(16.7)	(16.1)
No	63	70	83	63	74	85	438
	(81.8)	(76.9)	(92.2)	(77.8)	(91.4)	(83.3)	(83.9)
	77	91	90	81	81	102	
Total	(14.8)	(17.4)	(17.2)	(15.5)	(15.5)	(19.5)	522

Note. χ^2 (5, n = 522) = 13.75, p = .02. Cramér's V = .162.

Only 3 of the 20 commercial characteristics changed over time (Tables 48–50): principle female characters (χ^2 (5, n = 522) = 25.88, p = .01), principle characters playing the role of ordinary people (χ^2 (5, n = 522) = 14.17, p = .02), and presenter/spokesperson on camera (χ^2 (5, n = 522) = 13.75, p = .02). Principle characters as real people, principle characters animals, and real people in a minor role were excluded because of violation of the minimum expected cell-count assumption of chi-square. Principle female characters appeared more than expected in 2002 and 2003 but less than expected in 1999 and 2004. Principle character(s) actor

TABLE 50. EFFIE and Stewart and Furse proportion comparison.

Characteristic	EFFIE	Presence Stewart and Furse	Difference	SE	z
Humorous Tone	40.6%	5.3%	35.3%	0.019	18.58*
Brand-Differentiating Message	39.5%	44.4%	4.9%	0.026	1.88

*p < .05.

playing the role of an ordinary person was found less than expected only in 1999. Presenter/spokesperson on camera was found less than expected in 2001 and 2003, but more than expected in 2000.

Research Question 5: *Were there effective executional characteristic proportional differences between Stewart and Furse commercials and EFFIE commercials?*

We examined the proportional differences in effective characteristics found in the study by Stewart and Furse (1986) with those found in the EFFIE sample. Coded content in this study was compared with content coded in Stewart and Furse. We considered content effective if it showed a positive relationship to persuasion in addition to either recall and/or comprehension. In other words, for comparing characteristics, at least two of the three measured dependent variables in Stewart and Furse (1986) must have shown a positive relationship. This criterion yielded two characteristics common to both studies: brand-differentiating message and humorous tone (Table 51). Humorous tone ($z = 18.58$, $df = 1$, $p < .05$) was significantly more present in EFFIE (40.6%) compared to Stewart and Furse (5.3%). We discovered no statistically significant difference regarding the use of brand-differentiating messages.

CHAPTER 5

DISCUSSION
AND
CONCLUSIONS

REVIEW OF STUDY

Laskey et al. (1995) stated, "A commercial's effectiveness is likely to be influenced both by the intended message (the message strategy) and by how well that message is conveyed (the execution of the commercial message)" (p. 31). The goal of this research was to examine both the message strategy and commercial execution of television advertisements from EFFIE-award-winning campaigns from 1999 through 2004. This study differs from previous studies of this kind (Laskey et al., 1994, 1995; Stewart & Furse, 1986) since the sample covers 6 years of commercials from peer-reviewed effective campaigns. We called on message typologies of Laskey et al. (1989) and executional characteristics of Stewart and Furse (1986) to illustrate commercials descriptively, as well as to investigate research objectives. This chapter addresses the research findings and discusses the limitations, professional significance, and future research possibilities.

Descriptive Results
MRI product categories examined here contained a wide variety of products. Categories such as electronics, health and beauty aids, household products—food, and beverages comprised the largest sample contributors, ultimately making up half of the overall sample. Other important contributors included financial services, automotive, PSA-Nonprofit-Government, and travel products. The product categories included here exhibit a mix of durable, nondurable and service product categories. Stewart and Koslow (1989) suggested future research should examine consumer durables and service products. By using the EFFIE sample, these types of products were incorporated into measurement.

Ten advertising agency brands represented 53.4% of the entire sample. In addition, seven out of ten of these brands were also in the top ten in U.S. revenue as of 2004 (Adage, 2005). This finding could be a product of agency size, since agency brands with the highest revenue also do the most work and have the most offices. Furthermore, this finding could also confirm the findings of Schweitzer and Hester (1992) and Helgesen (1994), stating that recognition of work encourages creativity, increases industry prestige, and allows the agency further promotional accolades.

Based on the descriptive findings of the overall sample, the ideal EFFIE was created with characteristics receiving the highest frequency in each category. The ideal EFFIE commercial would be 30 seconds (85.6%) long and transformational (72.8%) with a major focus on user (29.7%) or brand (29.1%) image. The commercial would contain visual memory devices (99.4%), substantive supers (52.5%), as well as memorable rhymes, slogans, and mnemonic devices (79%). The main appeal would focus on product performance or benefit (29%) with a blind lead-in (29.3%) and a comedy format (25.1%). A brand-differentiating message will not be present (60.5%). The commercial would be set indoors (43.1%), contain music (83%), indirect comparisons (65.3%), and a humorous tone (40.6%). The commercial would contain principle male characters (62.5%) with actors playing the role of ordinary people (57.3%) and a background cast (57.3%).

Many commonalities and differences arise when comparing the ideal EFFIE to the dependent effectiveness measures found in Stewart and Furse (1986). The ideal EFFIE has four predominant characteristics related positively to persuasive measures: product performance or benefit as main appeal, indirect comparison, humorous tone, and actors playing the role of ordinary people. Interestingly enough, the ideal EFFIE exhibits two characteristics Stewart and Furse found negatively related to persuasion: principle character male and the use of a background cast. The EFFIE sample had almost no (3.1%) puffery. However, Stewart and Furse found the use of puffery effective in all three dependent measures. Most importantly, a high frequency of brand-differentiating messages failed to appear in the ideal EFFIE. Stewart and Furse stated, "Brand-differentiating message was, by far, the single most important executional factor for explaining both recall and persuasion for a product" (p. 23). Based on their findings, one would expect to see a high frequency of brand-differentiating messages in the overall

EFFIE sample. However, the ideal EFFIE does not support this notion.

Actually, the ideal EFFIE has many traits in common with the ideal Clio as described by Gagnard and Morris (1988). Both samples had:

- An actor playing an ordinary person
- Background cast
- Blind lead-ins
- Emotional appeals
- Humorous tone
- Indoor setting
- Principle male characters
- Heavy visual and audio memory devices

The use of substantive supers represented one point of difference with their presence in the Clio sample measured at 9.9% compared to their presence in over half of the EFFIE sample. Gagnard and Morris (1988) also found the presence of brand-differentiating messages to be less than 20% in their Clio sample. This is considerably less than the almost 40% found in the EFFIE sample.

In terms of message strategy, Laskey et al. (1995) found an overall higher percentage of informational compared to trans-formational strategies with preemptive message strategies being the most frequent. Comparing overall message strategy to effectiveness, measures found no significant difference in recall or persuasion measures (Laskey et al. used the same ARS-dependent variables as Stewart and Furse [1986]). Table 52 displays the ideal EFFIE with directional dependent outcomes from Stewart and Furse. In sum, the ideal EFFIE appears to exhibit some of the characteristics Stewart and Furse found effective as

TABLE 51. The ideal EFFIE and Stewart and Furse (1986) dependent measures.

Execution Characteristic	Ideal EFFIE (% present)	Recall	Comprehension	Persuasion
Spot Length	:30	NA	NA	NA
Visual Devices	Visual memory devices (99.4%)	+	+	0
	Substantive supers (52.5%)	–	–	0
Auditory Devices	Memorable rhymes, Slogans and mnemonic devices (79%)	+	+	0
Commercial Appeals	Product performance or benefit (29%)	–	+	+
Commercial Structures	Blind lead-in (29.3%)	0	0	0
Commercial Formats	Comedy (25.1%)	0	0	0
Brand-Differentiating Message	Not present (60.5%)	0	0	0
Message Typology	Transformational (72.8%)	ns	ns	ns
Message Typology Subtype	User image (29.7%)	ns	ns	ns
	Brand image (29.1%)	ns	ns	ns
Commercial Approach	More emotional (48.1)	+	0	0

(continued on next page)

TABLE 51. *(continued)*

Execution Characteristic	Ideal EFFIE (% present)	Recall	Comprehension	Persuasion
Commercial Setting	Indoors (43.1%)	0	+	0
Music	Music presence (83%)	+	0	0
Tone	Humorous tone (40.6%)	+	0	+
Comparison	Indirect comparison (65.3%)	0	0	+
Puffery	Not present (96.9%)	+	+	+
Commercial Characters	Principle male (62.5%)	–	–	–
	Actors playing the role of ordinary people (57.3%)	–	0	+
	Background cast (57.3%)	–	0	–

Note. + = Positive significant relationship in Stewart and Furse's (1986). – = Negative significant relationship in Stewart and Furse (1986). 0 = No significant relationship in Stewart and Furse (1986). NA = Not applicable. *ns* = Not significant according to Laskey et al. (1995).

well as traits that win Clio awards as examined by Gagnard and Morris (1988).

Congruency of FCB Grid in EFFIE Sample

The two hypotheses in this research tested the prediction strength of the FCB grid by examining how well EFFIE commercials exhibited their respected message typologies. The findings from these hypotheses offer minimal FCB grid predictive support. Products on the FCB grid were distributed as predicted in 2002 and 2003, which helped influence the statistical significance of the entire comparison. However, once these 2 years were removed, the significance of the relationship disappeared. Perhaps this evidence of a minimal relationship between thinking and feeling dimensions on the FCB grid and informational and transformational strategies from Laskey et al. (1989) point to the many criticisms noted by Rossiter et al. (1991). First, Rossiter et al. stated most advertisements demonstrate a balance between rational and emotional appeals. This was true in the EFFIE sample when examining the frequency of balance of rational and emotional (43.2%) commercial approach. Furthermore, while transformational commercials tended to be more congruent with the feeling dimension of the FCB grid, half of the FCB feeling product categories were classified as informational. Another reason for the lack of statistical support of this hypothesis could be because of Rossiter et al.'s claim the FCB grid does not differentiate between brand and product category. This argument contends the FCB grid unjustly combines product-category involvement and brand-choice involvement. Furthermore, evidence exists agreeing with Berger's (1986) hypothesis that emotion in advertising is on the increase since it is more difficult to differentiate a product based on informational characteristics. Overall, evidence presented here does not validate the FCB grid.

The Use of Informational and
Transformational Message Strategies by Year

Trends regarding the use of informational and transformational strategies as well as their respected message subcategories were examined over time. Commercials from EFFIE-award-winning campaigns exhibit an overall transformational message strategy. Each year of the sample indicates transformational strategies outnumbering informational ones. Likewise, the sample displays an upward trend in use of transformational message strategies. For example, in 1999 almost two-thirds (66.2%) of the commercials were transformational, but in 2003 (88.9%) and 2004 (87.2%) that had changed to almost 90%. EFFIE commercials now tend toward more transformational strategies.

This transformational strategy trend appears in the message subcategories as well. User image (31.5% overall) and brand image (30.7% overall) were the most present transformational strategies. Both remain somewhat consistent across years. The transformational strategy of use occasion (12.7%) was present in over 12% of the total sample, but growth of the strategy is noteworthy with only 4% presence in 1999 increasing to 22.7% in 2004. However, the use of informational trends such as USP (13.9% overall) and preemptive (11.1% overall) declined by year. The use of USP was present the most in 2000 with over 27% of the commercials displaying the strategy, but USP use shrunk to 4% in 2003 and 6% in 2004. Notably, USP was the only message strategy found positively related to persuasion measures (Laskey et al., 1995). Preemptive informational message strategies also saw their lowest use in 2003 and 2004. In conclusion, transformational messages dominate commercials from EFFIE-award-winning campaigns.

Product Category Message Typologies

We examined message typologies over time within product categories and found transformational strategies abundant across MRI product categories. In fact, in only two cases, automotive and travel, did message strategy statistically significantly deviate from its respected trend. Beverage, electronics, house products, food, PSA/nonprofit/government, and leisure/sports all demonstrated a consistent distribution of transformational message strategies over time. Health and beauty aids as well as financial products had a mix of message strategy distributions, but both skewed more toward transformational strategies in 2003 and 2004. No MRI product category in the EFFIE sample exhibited an overall informational message strategy. Furthermore, no product category tended toward informational message strategies in later years. The message strategy trend by product category is transformational.

Informational and Transformational
Executional Characteristics

An examination of the differences in executional characteristics between informational and transformational message manifest in commercials from EFFIE-award-winning campaigns led to numerous statistically significant differences.

Informational message strategy commercials were more likely to contain substantive supers visual devices, as well as have memorable rhymes, slogans, or mnemonic devices as auditory devices. Product performance or benefit as main message was a dominant appeal and associations were discovered with front-end impact or message-in-the-middle commercial structures. Informational ads showed a format association with testimonials by product users as well. Interestingly, informational commercials were associated with a balance of rational and emotional appeals rather than rational alone. This finding again agrees with Puto and Wells' (1984) and Rossiter et al.'s (1991) statements that ads typically mix rational and emotional approaches and is consistent with the findings of Frazer et al. (2002). In addition, informational message strategies were more associated with brand-differentiating messages as well as indirect product comparisons. Presenter/spokesperson on camera was the only dominant commercial characteristic associated more with informational message typologies. The dominance of brand-differentiating messages, indirect product comparisons, and presenter/spokesperson on camera show a propensity toward cognitive elements possibly related to central route attitude change as theorized by ELM (Petty et al., 1983). However, evidence presented here does not fully verify this assumption.

Only three dominant characteristics in the informational commercial profile negatively related to dependent measures, with none of the items negatively related to persuasion measures. Substantive supers and no commercial setting both negatively related to recall and comprehension, respectively. Memorable rhymes, slogans, or mnemonic devices, front-end impact structure, indirect comparisons, and brand-differentiating messages all contributed positively to one or all of Stewart and Furse's (1986) dependent measures. Table 53 displays the dominant characteristics of informative message typologies as well as their respected relationship to the dependent variables measured by Stewart and Furse.

Transformational typologies were not statistically associated with any particular visual or auditory device. Transformational strategies were associated with product reminder as main message, enjoyment as well as excitement/sensation/variety commercial appeals. They were more likely to use blind lead-in and humorous closing commercial structures and use a format focused on creating a mood or image. They were not associated statistically with brand-differentiating messages or comparisons.

TABLE **52.** Informative message typology and executional associations.

Execution Characteristic	EFFIE Informational Commercials	Recall	Comprehension	Persuasion
Visual Devices	Substantive supers	–	–	0
Auditory Devices	Memorable rhymes, slogans, or mnemonic devices	+	+	0
Commercial Appeals	Product performance or benefit as main message	–	+	0
Commercial Structures	Front-end impact	+	+	0
	Message in the middle	0	0	0
Commercial Formats	Testimonial by product user	0	0	0
Brand-Differentiating Message	Yes	+	+	+
Commercial Approach	Balance of rational and emotional	0	0	0
Commercial Setting	No setting	–	–	0
Music	ns	ns	ns	ns
Tone	ns	ns	ns	ns
Comparison	Indirect comparison	0	0	+
Puffery	ns	ns	ns	ns
Commercial Characters	Presenter/spokesperson on camera	0	0	0

Note. + = Positive significant relationship in Stewart and Furse's (1986). – = Negative significant relationship in Stewart and Furse's (1986). 0 = No significant relationship in Stewart and Furse (1986). *ns* = Not significant in EFFIE sample.

Transformational commercials were associated with an outdoor setting and used music as major element. Principle characters associated with transformational advertising included: principle male characters, principle racial or ethnic minority, the presence of a background cast, and racial or ethnic minorities in a minor role.

No dominant characteristics appeared in transformational messages positively contributing to persuasion. In fact, more factors contributed to negative persuasion as measured by Stewart and Furse (1986). These factors include: outdoor commercial setting, principle male characters, and the use of a background cast. Table 54 displays dominant transformational message typology executional associations as well as their respected impact on advertising effectiveness dependent variables as measured by Stewart and Furse (1986).

Executional Characteristic Trends
We explored executional characteristic trends occurring in the 1999 through 2004 EFFIE commercials, and although we discovered significant dependence by examining the use of characteristics by year, all associations were statistically weak. Executional characteristic relationships were caused by changes in single years among compared characteristics and were found to be without consistent trends. In other words, although findings indicate statically significant differences, the data lack practical significance. Moreover, although we made an effort to investigate these single-year changes, the general lack of trends and their isolation made any explanation problematic as to why one particular year would differ.

EFFIE and Stewart and Furse Differences
Finally, we examined the proportional differences in effective characteristics found in the study by Stewart and Furse (1986)

TABLE 53. Transformational message typology and executional associations.

Execution Characteristic	Transformational	Recall	Comprehension	Persuasion
Visual Devices	ns	ns	ns	ns
Auditory Devices	ns	ns	ns	ns
Commercial Appeals	Product reminder as main message	–	0	0
	Enjoyment appeals	+	0	0
	Excitement, sensation, variety	0	0	0
Commercial Structures	Blind lead-in	0	0	0
	Humorous closing	0	0	0
Commercial Formats	Creation of mood or image	0	0	0
Brand-Differentiating Message	ns	ns	ns	ns
Commercial Approach	ns	ns	ns	ns
Commercial Setting	Outdoors	+	0	–
Music	Music as a major element	+	0	0
Tone	ns	ns	ns	ns
Comparison	ns	ns	ns	ns
Puffery	ns	ns	ns	ns
Commercial Characters	Principle character male	–	–	–
	Principle character racial or ethnic minority	0	0	0
	Background cast	–	0	–
	Racial or ethnic minority character in a minor role	0	0	0

Note. + = Positive significant relationship in Stewart and Furse (1986). – = Negative significant relationship in Stewart and Furse (1986). 0 = No significant relationship in Stewart and Furse (1986). *ns* = Not significant in EFFIE sample.

and those manifested in the EFFIE sample. Effective characteristics from Stewart and Furse were chosen if they positively associated with persuasion and recall or message comprehension. Based on this criterion, we found only two characteristics common to both studies: humorous tone and the presence of a brand-differentiating message.

Humorous tone was the most frequent tone found in the EFFIE sample out of the available 17 tones, as well as being statistically proportionally different than tones found in Stewart and Furse (1986). Humorous tone was present in over 40% of the EFFIE sample. Yet, Stewart and Furse found humorous tones in just over 5% of their sample. No significant difference appeared in the presence of brand-differentiating messages between the two samples.

LIMITATIONS

Perhaps one of the most important discussion points of this research relates to the limitations experienced while conducting the analysis. Many of these limitations could not be avoided and future research should attempt to correct those that can be changed. In addition, measures of effectiveness examined by Stewart and Furse (1986), Stewart and Koslow (1989), as well as by Laskey et al. (1994) were measured for primarily nondurable products.

EFFIE Sample Limitations

The first limitation worthy of note relates specifically to the EFFIE sample used in this analysis. We purchased the original sample from the AMA, and the reels do not include silver or bronze winners prior to 1999. Unfortunately, this limited the sample size from the original intent. Initially, the years 1995 through 2004 were coded, yielding 670 total commercials. However, since logic would conclude some difference between award-level winners, the sample was truncated to compare only years with all award categories available.

Another issue regarding the sample involves the assignment of product categories. The EFFIE-award procedure occurs in two phases: overall judging of effectiveness briefs and then pooling briefs into product categories for final judging. Unfortunately, this pooling scenario changes the product category name from year to year. Although much of this change is subtle, it does cause an inconsistent product category naming scheme. For that reason, MRI categories were substituted. However, even with fewer product categories (40 to 25) much of the data richness of individual product categories gets lost.

Lastly, the EFFIE sample is made up only of commercials from advertising agencies willing to enter the competition. The large presence of top advertising agency brands in the sample could relate directly to the cost of entry as well as the politics winning an EFFIE award.

Coding Issues

Coding for this project was conducted over a 2-year period. A team effort by sixteen coders contributed to the findings of this research and data collection. The authors trained the coders to the best of their ability and took care to produce the most reliable data possible. However, there arose coding limitations worth mentioning which could be examined and possibly controlled in future research situations. Primarily, these coding situations have to do with understanding Stewart and Furse's (1986) terminology, the mutual exclusivity of categories, and the general challenge of coding latent typologies.

Coders struggled when judging some of the executional characteristics used by Stewart and Furse (1986) because of the terminology, as well as dated examples within the definitions. Coders for this project were junior- and senior-level advertising majors. Since they were all advertising students, they were still in the process of learning advertising terminology. Reliability scores suffered because of this confusion of terms (such as visual tagline). Even though the primary researcher acknowledged these discrepancies in terminology during the training meetings, the effort to clear the confusion proved fruitless. As a result, this forced the primary researcher to make corrections when needed while settling latent variable coding disputes.

Dated examples in the codebook, as well as vague descriptive definitions also possibly led to less-than-pristine intercoder reliability scores. For example, the definition of substantive supers (as mentioned earlier), follows: A superscript (words on the screen) used to reinforce some characteristic of the product or a part of the commercial message–for example, 50% stronger," "3 out of 4 doctors recommend." The first part of the definition actually stated, "A superscript (words on the screen) used to reinforce some characteristic of the product or a part of the commercial message" is appropriate and easy to understand. However, the examples: "for example, 50% stronger," "3 out of 4 doctors recommend" caused many of the coders to miscode subtle words on screen, ultimately reducing the reliability of a manifest content category.

Vague definitions also caused manifest content-coding discrepancies. Take for example, the largest violator: Principal character(s) actor playing role of ordinary person. This commercial character category received a Perreault and Leigh reliability index score of .34; the lowest of all measured categories. This low-reliability results from the definition provided by the Stewart and Furse (1986) codebook simply stating, "Must be delivering the major portion of the message." In other words, the title of the category is the definition. Again, coders received an interpretation of this category in detail during coding training, but reliability still suffered. To remedy this, the primary researcher settled disagreements and recoded this category for each commercial.

All other low-intercoder reliabilities related to the coding of latent content. No matter how well categories are defined, the very nature of latent content remains subjective and cognitively involving. Some of the lowest Perreault and Leigh reliability scores occurred in latent categories such as commercial appeals or selling propositions (.54), commercial format (.61), message typology (.67), message typology subtype (.56), rational or emotional appeal (.55), and commercial tone (.65). One reason reliability in these categories suffered was because of the number of choices available. For example, commercial appeals or selling propositions contains 13 coding choices. Commercial format contains 18 coding choices. Commercial tone contains 17 coding choices. Having so many choices in one particular category increases the judge's cognitive load. In addition, many of the commercials have characteristics consistent with more than one variable in a category, which also increases the subjectivity of the data. For example, if a commercial begins indoors and then moves outdoors, which setting selection should the coder choose? Perhaps using more coders could have remedied this problem, such as the five-coder scenario used by Laskey et al. (1994). Even with these limitations, we made an effort to maintain confidence in the data, as well as the findings, as high as scientifically possible.

Finally, one should use caution when assessing the impact of dependent measures on executional variables as reported by Stewart and Furse (1986). The overall direction of impact was used in this study. However, they report "no single executional factor accounted for more than 6% of the variance of any measure" and suggested, "care should be exercised when interpreting simple item-by-item relationships" (p. 21).

Future Research

This exploratory study is ripe for future research. Most importantly, this research provides a U.S. benchmark for future examinations of advertising differences in message strategy and appeals between cultures. Furthermore, many other possibilities are available. First, this study could represent the beginning of a longer longitudinal study. For example, researchers could add EFFIE winners from future years to monitor advertising trends. Likewise, adding future years would further improve the depth and richness of product category and message typology subtype analysis missing here because of the limited sample. Second, a comparison with a random sample of nonwinners would inform the question how or if EFFIE winners differentiate from non-winners. Third, an investigation into the differences between Clio or other creative award competitions and the EFFIEs would be telling. This type of investigation could address the similarities and differences between creative and effective awards as judged by industry peers. Lastly, findings from this study as well as from the future research possibilities previously mentioned could serve as a stimulus framework for examining specific advertising independent and dependent effectiveness measures.

Future research should also take into consideration the methodological challenges this research presented. Updating the Stewart and Furse (1986) instrument with current examples as well as following the reliability estimation processes established here should improve the quality of future studies.

CONCLUSION

No other robust sample of advertising from effective campaigns exists like the EFFIE awards. Although the sample suffers limitations and does not indicate specific effective measures, the EFFIE sample does provide a practitioner-reviewed framework of advertising originating from effective campaigns.

Findings from this exploratory research strongly contribute to advertising effectiveness literature. EFFIE commercials exhibit some characteristics found to contribute positively to dependent measures used by Stewart and Furse (1986). However, many differences exist, specifically with the presence (or absence) of brand-differentiating messages in EFFIE advertising. In addition, EFFIE ads show a definite trend toward more transformational message strategies, specifically in terms of user and brand image with use occasion on the increase as well. Importantly, this exhibits a departure from informational focused ads. Perhaps advertising now tends to more emotion-based, image-focused appeals as stated by Berger (1986). Furthermore, perhaps this signifies a sea change to more value-expressive appeals, even across product categories typically considered utilitarian (Johar & Sirgy, 1991).

The research presented here also investigated the face validity of the FCB grid but discovered minimal support. Findings presented here offer a starting point for further theoretical testing of the FCB grid.

Appendix A

Coding Sheet

EFFIE AWARD WINNING ADVERTISING PROJECT Coding Sheet

V1 Case ID# _____ **V2** Coder initials _____

V3 Agency Name (EFFIE):

_____

PRINT NEATLY

V4 Brand (EFFIE): _____

_____

PRINT NEATLY

V5 Ad Title (EFFIE): _____

_____

PRINT NEATLY

V6 Spot Time (EFFIE): (1) :30   (2) :60   (3) Other___

V7 Color (EFFIE):   (1) All Color (2) B & W (3) Mixed

V8 Award Level (EFFIE): (1) Gold   (2) Silver   (3) Bronze

V9 Award Year (EFFIE):

(1) 2004	(4) 2001	(7) 1998	(10) 1995
(2) 2003	(5) 2000	(8) 1997	
(3) 2002	(6) 1999	(9) 1996	

V10 Award Category (EFFIE):

(1) Agricultural/Industrial/   (2) Alcoholic Beverages
    Building   (3) Apparel and Accessories

(4) Automobiles & Vehicles
(5) Beauty Aids
(6) Beverages/ Alcohol Spirits
(7) Beverages/Beer
(8) Beverages/Carbonated
(9) Beverages/Noncarbonated
(10) Breakfast Foods
(11) Business Products
(12) Children's Products
(13) Computer & Related for Business/Personal Purposes
(14) Consumer Electronics
(15) Cosmetics
(16) Credit/Debit Cards
(17) Delivery Systems and Products
(18) Entertainment
(19) "Fashion, Apparel, and Accessories"
(20) Fast Food and Restaurants
(21) Financial Services/Products
(22) General Retail/E-tail
(23) Health Aids
(24) Health Aids/ Over-the-counter Products
(25) Health Aids/ Prescription Products
(26) Health and Medical Products and Services
(27) Hotels and Resorts
(28) Household Durable Products
(29) Industrial/Building Products and Services
(30) Internet Services
(31) Leisure Products
(32) New Product or Services Introductions** (**re-classify to a specific product category)
(33) "Nonalcoholic, Carbonated Beverages"
(34) Package Food/Regular
(35) Personal Care Products
(36) Pet Care
(37) Professional Services
(38) Real Estate
(39) Retail
(40) Self Care: Body
(41) Snacks/Desserts/ Confections
(42) Specialized Retail/E-tail
(43) TeleCom Services
(44) Transportation
(45) Travel and Tourism

If category is not listed or confusing, please write it here: ___

A. Visual Devices (Frazer et al., 2002; Gagnard & Morris, 1988; Stewart & Furse, 1986; Stewart & Koslow, 1989)

V11: Scenic beauty

(1) Presence
(2) Absence
(3) Cannot code

V15: Surrealistic visuals

(1) Presence
(2) Absence
(3) Cannot code

V12: Beautiful characters

(1) Presence
(2) Absence
(3) Cannot code

V16: Substantive supers

(1) Presence
(2) Absence
(3) Cannot code

V13: Ugly characters

(1) Presence
(2) Absence
(3) Cannot code

V17: Visual tagline

(1) Presence
(2) Absence
(3) Cannot code

V14: Graphic display

(1) Presence
(2) Absence
(3) Cannot code

V18: Visual memory device

(1) Presence
(2) Absence
(3) Cannot code

B. Auditory Devices (Frazer et al., 2002; Gagnard & Morris, 1988; Stewart & Furse, 1986; Stewart & Koslow, 1989)

V19: Memorable rhymes, slogans or mnemonic devices:

(1) Presence
(2) Absence
(3) Cannot code

V20: Unusual sound effects

(1) Presence
(2) Absence
(3) Cannot code

V21: Spoken tagline

(1) Presence
(2) Absence
(3) Cannot code

C. Commercial Appeals or Selling Propositions (Stewart & Furse, 1986; Gagnard & Morris, 1988; Stewart & Koslow, 1989; Frazer et al., 2002)

V22: What is the dominant commercial appeal or selling proposition?
  (1) Attribute or ingredients as main message
  (2) Product performance or benefit as main message
  (3) Psychological or subjective benefits as main message
  (4) Product reminder as main message
  (5) Sexual appeal
  (6) Comfort appeals
  (7) Safety appeals
  (8) Enjoyment appeals
  (9) Welfare appeals
  (10) Social approval
  (11) Self-esteem or self-image
  (12) Achievement
  (13) Excitement, sensation, variety

D. Commercial Structures (Frazer et al., 2002; Gagnard & Morris, 1988; Stewart & Furse, 1986; Stewart & Koslow, 1989)

V23: What is the dominant commercial structure?
  (1) Front-end impact
  (2) Surprise or suspense in the middle
  (3) Surprise or suspense at closing
  (4) Unusual setting or situation
  (5) Humorous closing
  (6) Blind lead-in
  (7) Message in the middle (doughnut)

E. Commercial Format (Frazer et al., Patti, 2002; Gagnard & Morris, 1988; Stewart & Furse, 1986; Stewart & Koslow, 1989)

V24: What is the dominant commercial format of the commercial?

(1) Vignette
(2) Continuity of action
(3) Slice of life
(4) Testimonial by product user
(5) Endorsement by celebrity or authority
(6) Announcement
(7) Demonstration of product in use or by analogy
(8) Demonstration of results of using product
(9) Comedy or satire
(10) Animation/cartoon/ rotoscope
(11) Photographic stills
(12) Creation of mood or image as dominant element
(13) Commercial written as serious drama
(14) Fantasy, exaggeration or surrealism as dominant element
(15) Problem and solution (before/after presentation)
(16) Interview (person on the street or elsewhere)
(17) Camera involves audience in situation
(18) New wave (product graphics)

F. Typology of Broadcast Commercial Messages (Frazer et al., 2002; Laskey et al., 1989, 1995; Ramapradasad & Hasegawa, 1992; Yssel & Gustafson, 1998)

V25: Informational/Rational OR Transformational/ Image/Emotional

(1) Informational (If yes, go to V26 and select the best overall answer from only choices 1–6)
(2) Transformational (If yes, go to V26 and select the best over all answer from only choices 7–11)

V26: Informational/Transformational Subcategories
Informational

(1) Comparative (show or explicitly mention competing brands)
(2) Unique Selling Proposition (explicit claims or assertions of uniqueness)
(3) Preemptive (factually based but no claim of uniqueness or mention of competition)
(4) Hyperbole (built around exaggerated or extravagant claims)
(5) Generic-Info (factual messages focused on product class)
(6) Other (informational but not included above, please describe) _____

Transformational

(7) User Image (focus on the users of a brand and their lifestyles)
(8) Brand Image (image of brand itself such as quality, prestige and/or status)
(9) Use Occasion (focus on the experience of using the brand)
(10) Generic-Trans (image of product class)
(11) Other (transformational but not included above, please describe) _____

G. Commercial Approach (Frazer et al., 2002; Gagnard & Morris 1988; Stewart & Furse 1986; Stewart & Koslow 1989)

V27: Rational or emotional appeal?

(1) More rational
(2) Balance of rational and emotional
(3) More emotional

V28: Brand-differentiating message

(1) Presence   (3) Cannot code

(2) Absence

H. Commercial Setting (Frazer et al., 2002; Gagnard & Morris, 1988; Stewart & Furse, 1986; Stewart & Koslow, 1989)

V29: Where is the dominant commercial setting?

(1) Indoors   (3) Other

(2) Outdoors   (4) No setting

V30: Where is the commercial setting?

(1) Urban apartment/housing   (5) Foreign locale/

(2) Rural apartment/housing   landmark

(3) Generic office/business   (6) Green pasture

    setting   (7) Mountainous area

(4) Generic restaurant   (8) Other _____

    setting   (9) Not applicable

I. Music (Frazer et al., 2002 [artist added for research interest]; Gagnard & Morris, 1988; Stewart & Furse, 1986; Stewart & Koslow, 1989)

V31: Presence or absence of music in commercials

(1) Presence   (2) Absence

V32: Presence or absence of music as a major element

(1) Presence   (2) Absence

V33: Music Artist (Added Music Interest)

(1) Identifiable—Who? _____ (2) Unidentifiable

V34: Music style in commercials

(1) Alternative, Contemporary Hits, Rock (4) Jazz

(2) Classical   (5) Urban

(3) Country   (6) Unidentifiable

V35: Is the music a brand jingle?

(1) Presence   (2) Absence

J. Commercial Tone and Atmosphere (Frazer et al., 2002; Gagnard & Morris, 1988; Stewart & Furse, 1986; Stewart & Koslow, 1989)

V36: (Please select the predominant tone)

(1) Cute/adorable
(2) Hard sell
(3) Warm and caring
(4) Modern/contemporary
(5) Wholesome/healthy
(6) Technological/futuristic
(7) Conservative/traditional
(8) Old fashioned/nostalgic
(9) Happy/fun-loving
(10) Cool/laid-back
(11) Somber/serious
(12) Uneasy/tense/ irritated
(13) Relaxed/ comfortable
(14) Glamorous
(15) Humorous
(16) Suspenseful
(17) Rough/rugged

K. Comparisons (Frazer et al., 2002; Gagnard & Morris, 1988; Stewart & Furse, 1986; Stewart & Koslow, 1989)

V37: Is there a direct comparison with other products?

(1) yes   (2) no

V38: Is there an indirect comparison with other products?

(1) yes   (2) no

V39: Is there puffery, or unsubstantiated claim made?

(1) yes   (2) no

L. Hero Coding (added interest)

V40: Main character in the spot is/becomes a hero

(1) yes
(2) no

V41: Brand in the spot is/becomes a hero

(1) yes
(2) no

M. Commercial Characters (Frazer et al., 2002; Gagnard & Morris, 1988; Stewart & Furse, 1986; Stewart & Koslow, 1989)

V42: Principle character(s) male?

(1) yes
(2) no

V47: Principle character(s) actor playing role of ordinary person?

(1) yes
(2) no

V43: Principle character(s) female?

(1) yes
(2) no

V48: Principle character(s) real people?

(1) yes
(2) no

V44: Principle character(s) child or infant?

(1) yes
(2) no

V49: Principle character(s) creation?

(1) yes
(2) no

V45: Principle character(s) racial or ethnic minority?

(1) yes
(2) no

V50: Principle character(s) animal?

(1) yes
(2) no

V46: Principle character(s) celebrity?

(1) yes
(2) no

V51: Principle character(s) animated?

(1) yes
(2) no

V52: No principle character(s)?

(1) yes
(2) no

V53: Characters identified with company?

(1) yes
(2) no

V54: Background cast (others walking, etc)?

(1) yes
(2) no

V55: Racial or ethnic minority character in minor role?

(1) yes
(2) no

V56: Celebrity in minor role (cameo appearance)?

(1) yes
(2) no

V57: Animal(s) in minor role?

(1) yes
(2) no

V58: Created character or cartoon characters in minor role?

(1) yes
(2) no

V59: Real person in minor role (not professional actors)?

(1) yes
(2) no

V60: Recognized continuing character?

(1) yes
(2) no

V61: Presenter/spokesperson on camera?

(1) yes
(2) no

Any other comments or observations?

APPENDIX B

OPERATIONAL DEFINITIONS

EFFIE Coding Categories and Operational Definitions

A. Visual Devices (Frazer et al., 2002; Gagnard & Morris, 1988; Stewart & Furse, 1986; Stewart & Koslow, 1989)

- **Scenic beauty:** Does the commercial present striking scenes of natural beauty (mountains, flowing streams) at some point?
- **Beauty of characters:** Does the commercial present one or more strikingly beautiful people?
- **Ugliness of characters:** Does the commercial present one or more striking ugly characters?
- **Graphic display:** Does the commercial use graphic displays or charts as part of its presentation? Such graphic may be computer generated.
- **Surrealistic visuals:** Does the commercial present unreal visuals, distorted visuals, fantastic scenes like a watch floating through outer space?
- **Substantive supers:** A superscript (words on the screen) used to reinforce some characteristic of the product or a part of the commercial message—for example, 50% stronger," "3 out of 4 doctors recommend."
- **Visual tagline:** A visually presented statement of new information at the end of the commercial; for example, the screen shows the name of participating dealers or another product that was not the focus of the commercial shown. Corporate logos or slogans do not qualify.

- **Use of visual memory device:** Any devices shown that reinforce product benefit, the product name, or the message delivered by the commercial—for example, time-release capsules bouncing in the air, the word *Jello* spelled out with Jello Gelatin.

B. Auditory Devices (Frazer et al., 2002; Gagnard & Morris, 1988; Stewart & Furse, 1986; Stewart & Koslow, 1989)

- **Memorable rhymes, slogans, or mnemonic devices:** Non-musical rhymes or other mnemonics may be incorporated in lyrics of a song, but must also stand alone, apart from music.
- **Unusual sound effects:** Out of place, unusual, or bizarre use of sound— for example, the sound of a jackhammer as someone eats a pretzel.
- **Spoken tagline:** A statement at the end of the commercial that presents new information usually unrelated to the principal focus of the commercial—for example, "And try new lime flavor, too."

C. Commercial Appeals or Selling Proposition (Frazer et al., 2002; Gagnard & Morris, 1988; Stewart & Furse, 1986; Stewart & Koslow, 1989)

What is the dominant commercial appeal or selling proposition?

- **Attribute or ingredients as main message:** A major focus of the commercial is to communicate something about how the product is made (for example, car in manufacturing) or ingredients (for example, the only toothpaste with stannous fluoride).
- **Product performance or benefits as main message:** A major focus of the commercial is to communicate what

the product does (for example, shinier tub, fresher breath, whiter teeth) or how to use it.

- **Psychological or subjective benefits of product ownership:** A major focus of the commercial is to communicate hidden or nonprovable benefits of having/using the product (for example, "you'll be more popular, sexier, or more confident").
- **Product reminder as main message:** The product or package is the primary message rather than any specific attribute or benefit of use.
- **Sexual appeal:** Main focus of commercial is on sexual cues.
- **Comfort appeals:** Main focus of commercial is on cues appealing to creature comforts (soft chairs, cool climate).
- **Safety appeals:** Main focus of commercial is on cues appealing to being free from fear or physical danger.
- **Enjoyment appeals:** Main focus of commercial is on cues about enjoying life to the fullest, having good food and drink, and so on.
- **Welfare appeals:** Main focus is on caring or providing for others (for example, gift giving).
- **Social approval:** Main focus of commercial is on belonging, winning friends, obtaining approval of others.
- **Self-esteem or self-image:** Main focus of commercial is on feeling better about oneself, improving oneself, being a better person.
- **Achievement:** Main focus of commercial is on obtaining superiority over others, getting ahead, winning.
- **Excitement, sensation, variety:** Main focus of commercial is on adding excitement, thrills, and variety to life and avoiding boredom.

D. Commercial Structure (Frazer et al., 2002; Gagnard & Morris, 1988; Stewart & Furse, 1986; Stewart & Koslow, 1989)

What is the dominant commercial structure?

- **Front-end impact:** The first 10 seconds of the commercial creates suspense, questions, surprise, drama, or something that otherwise gains attention.
- **Surprise or suspense in middle of commercial:** Something surprising, dramatic, or suspenseful occurs in the middle of the commercial.
- **Surprise or suspense at closing:** Commercial ends with a surprise, an unexpected event, suspense, or drama.
- **Unusual setting or situation:** Product is in setting not normally associated with product purchase or use-for example, a car on top of a mountain, a contemporary wine in ancient Greece.
- **Humorous closing:** Commercial ends with a joke, pun, witticism, or slapstick.
- **Blind lead-in:** No identification of product until the end of the commercial.
- **Message in the middle (doughnut):** Music and/or action at the start and close of commercial with announcer copy in the middle—for example, Green Giant commercials.

E. Commercial Format (Frazer et al., 2002; Gagnard & Morris, 1988; Stewart & Furse, 1986; Stewart & Koslow, 1989)

What is the dominant commercial format of the commercial?

- **Vignettes:** A series of two or more stories that could stand alone; no continuing storyline but several independent stories (which may convey the same message). Multiple interviews would be an example. Has no continuity of action.

- **Continuity of action:** Commercial has a single storyline throughout with an obvious beginning, middle, and end; a common theme, character, or issue ties the whole commercial together from beginning to end. This may be an interview with a single individual, slice of life, or any other format that involves continuity of action.
- **Slice of life:** An interplay between two or more people that portrays a conceivable real-life situation. There is continuity of action.
- **Testimonial by product user:** One or more individuals recounts his or her satisfaction with the product advertised or the results of using the product advertised—for example, Bill Cosby for Jello Pudding.
- **Endorsement by celebrity or authority:** One or more individuals (or organizations) advocates or recommends the product but does not claim personal use of satisfaction.
- **Announcement:** Commercial's format is that of a newscast or sportscast sales announcement.
- **Demonstration of product in use or by analogy:** A demonstration of the product in use-for example, a man shaving in a commercial for shaving lather, women applying makeup. A demonstration of the use of the product, benefit, or product characteristic by an analogy or device rather than actual demonstration.
- **Demonstration of results of using product:** Demonstration of the outcome of using the product—for example, shining floors, bouncing hair.
- **Comedy or satire:** The commercial is written as a comedy, parody, or satire. Not only is humor an element of the commercial, but also the commercial is written to be funny.
- **Animation/cartoon/rotoscope:** The entire commercial or some substantial part of the commercial is animated.

A rotoscope is a combination of real life and animation on the screen at the same time—for example, the Trix Rabbit.

- **Photographic stills:** The use of photographic stills in part of the commercial. These may be product shots, settings, or models.
- **Creation of mood or image as dominant element:** An attempt to create a desire for the product, without offering a specific product claim by appealing to the viewer's emotional/sensory involvement. The primary thrust of the commercial is the creation of a feeling or mood.
- **Commercial written as serious drama:** The commercial is written as a stage play, melodrama, or tragedy.
- **Fantasy, exaggeration, or surrealism as dominant element:** The use of animation or other visual device instead of a realistic treatment to suspend disbelief or preclude literal translation on the part of the viewer.
- **Problem and solution (before/after presentation):** An attempt to define or show a problem, then indicate how the product eliminates or reduces the problem.
- **Interview (person on the street or elsewhere):** An interview (Q&A) is a primary vehicle in the commercial.
- **Camera involves audience in situation:** Use of camera as eyes of viewer. Camera creates participation in commercial.
- **New wave (product graphics):** Use of posterlike visuals, fast cuts, high symbolism as in Diet Pepsi.

F. Typology of Broadcast Commercial Messages (Frazer et al., 2002; Laskey et al., 1989, 1995; Ramapradasad & Hasegawa, 1992; Yssel & Gustafson, 1998)

Is main message informational (rational or cognitive) or transformational (image, emotional or feeling)?

G. Informational/Transformational Subcategories (Frazer et al., 2002; Laskey et al., 1989, 1995; Ramapradasad & Hasegawa, 1992; Yssel & Gustafson, 1998)

Informational Subcategory

- **Comparative:** Testable claim of uniqueness or superiority and explicitly mentioning the competition.
- **Unique Selling Proposition:** Explicit testable claim of uniqueness or superiority.
- **Preemptive:** Testable claim based on an attribute or benefit without claim of uniqueness or explicit mention of competition.
- **Hyperbole:** Untestable claim based upon an attribute or benefit.
- **Informational Generic:** Message focuses upon the product class.
- **Informational Other:** Any informational ad not classified above.

Transformational subcategory

- **User Image:** Message focuses on the brand user.
- **Brand Image:** Message focuses on developing a brand personality.
- **Use Occasion:** Message focuses on usage occasions appropriate for the brand.
- **Transformational Generic:** Message focuses on product class.
- **Transformational Other:** Any transformational ad not classified above.

H. Commercial Approach (Frazer et al., 2002; Gagnard & Morris, 1988; Stewart & Furse, 1986; Stewart & Koslow, 1989)

Rational or Emotional?

- **Rational approach:** A fairly straightforward presentation of the product's attributes and claims.
- **Emotional approach:** An emotional appeal does not appeal to reason but to feelings.
- **Balance of rational and emotional:** An appeal counterpoising rational and emotional.

Brand- differentiating message?

- **Brand-differentiating message:** Is the principle message of the commercial unique to the product being advertised, or could any product make this claim? The commercial must make it clear that the message is unique; that is, the commercial must explicitly indicate the uniqueness or difference of the product.

I. Commercial Setting (Frazer et al., 2002; Gagnard & Morris, 1988; Stewart & Furse, 1986; Stewart & Koslow, 1989)

- **Indoor:** Is the commercial setting, or a significant part of it, indoors or in other human-made structures (for example, a kitchen, garage, office, stadium, airplane)?
- **Outdoors:** Is the commercial setting, or a significant part of it, outdoors (mountain, rivers, backyard, garden, or other natural setting)? Do not include unnatural environments such as stadium or home driveway.
- **Other:** Not indoor or outdoor.
- **No setting:** There is no particular setting for the commercial; the setting is neutral, neither indoor nor outdoors.

J. Music (Frazer et al., 2002 [unless otherwise noted]; Gagnard & Morris, 1988; Stewart & Furse, 1986; Stewart & Koslow, 1989)

- **Music:** Is music present in the commercial in any form?
- **Music as a major element:** Do the lyrics or the focus of the music used in the commercial carry a product message?
- **Music Artist:** Is the artist identifiable, if so, who? (variable added by author)
- **Music style:** What is the music genre? (variable added by author)
- Is the music a brand jingle? (variable added by author)

K. Commercial Tone and Atmosphere (Frazer et al., 2002; Gagnard & Morris, 1988; Stewart & Furse, 1986; Stewart & Koslow, 1989)

- **Choices include:** cute/adorable, hard sell, warm/caring, modern/contemporary, wholesome/healthy, technological/futuristic, conservative/traditional, old fashioned/nostalgic, happy/fun-loving, cool/laid-back, somber/serious, uneasy/tense/irritated, relaxed/comfortable, glamorous, humorous, suspenseful, rough/rugged.

L. Comparisons (Frazer et al., 2002; Gagnard & Morris, 1988; Stewart & Furse, 1986; Stewart & Koslow, 1989)

- **Is there a direct comparison with other products?** A competitor is identified by name. May also be a direct comparison with an old version of the product advertised.
- **Is there an indirect comparison with other products?** A comparison is made between the advertised product and a competitor, but the competitor is not named.

- **Is there puffery, or are unsubstantiated claims made?**
  Product is declared best, better, finest without identification of dimension or attribute.

M. Hero Coding

Is main character in spot is/becomes a hero?

Brand in spot is/becomes a hero?

N. Commercial Characters (Frazer et al., 2002; Gagnard & Morris, 1988; Stewart & Furse, 1986; Stewart & Koslow, 1989)

- **Principal character(s) male:** The character(s) carrying the major on-camera role of delivering the commercial message is a male. Incidental, background on-camera appearance is not applicable.
- **Principal character(s) female:** The character(s) carrying the major on-camera role of delivering the commercial message is a female. Incidental, background on-camera appearance is not applicable.
- **Principal character(s) child or infant:** The character(s) carrying the major on-camera role of delivering the commercial message is a child or infant. Incidental, background on-camera appearance is not applicable.
- **Principal character(s) racial or ethnic minority:** One or more of the principal on-camera characters is black, Hispanic, Oriental, or of some other clearly identifiable minority.
- **Principal character(s) celebrity:** The character(s) delivering the major portion of the message on camera is well known either by name or face. Celebrities may be athletes, movie stars or well-known corporate Tables (but not simply the identified head of a corporation).

- **Principal character(s) actor playing role of ordinary person:** Must be delivering the major portion of the message.
- **Principal character(s) real people:** Are one or more of the principal characters identified as real people (as opposed to actors playing a role)? This may take the form of a hidden camera or an interview.
- **Principal character(s) creation:** The principal character is a created role, person, or cartoon Table—for example, Ronald McDonald, Pillsbury Doughboy.
- **Principal character(s) animal:** Is one or more of the principal characters an animal (either real or animated)?
- **Principal character(s) animated:** Is one or more of the principal characters animated (cartoon)?
- **No principal character(s):** No central character or set of characters delivers a major portion of the commercial message, although there may be characters performing roles on camera relevant to the message.
- **Characters identified with company:** Is one or more of the characters in the commercial symbolic of or well identified with the company manufacturing and/or distributing the product? The character may be real, created, or animated but should be identified with the company, not a specific product—for example, Keebler Elves, Green Giant.
- **Background cast:** Are there people in the commercial other than the principal characters, people who serve as scenery or background—for example, people walking by, people sitting in a bar. These people are only incidental to the commercial message—that is, not active in making a product claim or demonstrating a product benefit.
- **Celebrity in minor role (cameo appearance)**
- **Animal(s) in minor role**
- **Created character or cartoon characters in minor role**

- **Real person in minor role:** May be actual consumers (specifically identified) or employees.
- **Recognized continuing character:** Is one or more of the principle or minor characters in the commercial recognized as a part of a continuing advertising campaign? Is the character associated with the product by virtue of previous appearances in commercials for the product?
- **Presenter/spokesperson on camera:** Is the audio portion of the commercial message delivered by voice-over announcer (person not on camera), character(s) on camera, or a combination of both?

REFERENCES

Aaker, D., & Norris, D. (1982). Characteristics of TV commercials perceived as informative. *Journal of Advertising Research, 22*(3), 61–70.

Abernethy, A. M., & Franke, G. R. (1996). The information content of advertising: A meta-analysis. *Journal of Advertising, 25*(2), 1–17.

Abraham, D. A., Batra, R., & Myers, J. G. (1990). Getting the most out of advertising and promotion. *Harvard Business Review, 68*, 50–60.

Albers-Miller, N. D., & Starfford, M. R. (1999). International services advertising: An examination of the variation in appeal use for experiential and utilitarian services. *Journal of Services Marketing, 13*(4), 390–406.

Alexander, A., Benjamin, L. M., Hoerrner, K., & Roe, D. (1998). "We'll be back in a moment": A content analysis of advertisements in children's television in the 1950s. *Journal of Advertising, 27*(3), 1–9.

Allen, C. T., & Janiszewski, C. A. (1989, February). Assessing the role of contingency awareness in attitudinal conditioning with implications for advertising research. *Journal of Marketing Research, 26*, 30–43.

Al-Olayan, F. S., & Kirande, K. (2000). A content analysis of magazine advertisements from the United States and the Arab World. *Journal of Advertising, 29*(3), 69–82.

Arens, W. F. (2004). *Contemporary advertising* (9th ed.). New York: McGraw-Hill Irwin.

ARF. (2005). *ARF, AAAA, and ANA pursue measurement for consumer engagement to complement consumer exposure metrics.* Retrieved October 6, 2006, from http://www.arfsite.org

Azzaro, M. (2004). *Strategic media decisions.* Chicago: The Copy Workshop.

Baker, W. E., & Lutz, R. J. (2000). An empirical test of an updated relevance accessibility model of advertising effectiveness. *Journal of Advertising, 29,* 1–14.

Barry, T. E. (1987). The development of the hierarchy of effects: An historical perspective. *Current Issues and Research in Advertising, 2,* 251–295.

Barry, T. E., & Howard, D. J. (1990). A review and critique of the hierarchy of effects in advertising. *International Journal of Advertising, 9,* 121–135.

Bass, F. M., & Clarke, D. G. (1972). Testing distributed lag models of advertising effect. *Journal of Marketing Research, 3,* 298–308.

Berelson, B. (1952). *Content analysis in communication research.* Glencoe, IL: Free Press.

Berger, D. (1986). Theory into practice: The FCB grid. *European Research, 14*(1), 35–46.

Bettman, J. R. (1979). *An information processing theory of consumer choice.* Reading, MA: Addison-Wesley.

Bogart, L. (1976). Mass advertising: The message, not the measure. *Harvard Business Review, 54,* 107–116.

Browne, B. A. (1998). Gender stereotypes in advertising on children's television in the 1990s: A cross-national analysis. *Journal of Advertising, 27*(1), 83–96.

Caplan, J. (2006, January 23). 5,000 Channels: TV on the Internet. *Time, 167*(4).

Childs, N., & Maher, J. K. (2003). Gender in food advertising to children: Boys eat first. *British Food Journal, 105*(7), 408–419.

Clynes, M. (1980). The communication of emotion: theory of sentics. In R. Plutchik & H. Kellerman (Eds.), *Emotion: Theory, research and experience, Vol. 1: Theories of emotion.* New York: Academic Press.

Cohen, J. (1960). A coefficient of agreement for nominal scales. *Educational and Psychological Measurement, 20*, 37–46.

Colley, R. H. (1961). *Defining advertising goals for measured advertising results.* New York: Association of National Advertisers.

Consoli, J. (2005, December 19). MindShare: Consumers buy DVRs to skip ads. *MediaWeek.*

Consoli, J. (2006, February 27). Closing the loop. *MediaWeek.*

Cook, W. A., & Kover, A. J. (1997). Research and the meaning of advertising effectiveness. In W. D. Wells (Ed.), *Measuring advertising effectiveness* (pp. 13–20). Mahwah, NJ: LEA.

Crask, M. R., & Laskey, H. A. (1990). A positioning-based decision model for selecting advertising messages. *Journal of Advertising Research, 30*(4), 32–37.

Creamer, M. (2006). *ARF reveals working definition of engagement.* Retrieved January 3, 2007, from http://adage.com/news.coms?newsld=48362

Creamer, M., & Arndorfer, J. B. (2005, June 13). Leo Burnett chief chides creatives over EFFIE apathy. *Advertising Age.*

Dichter, E. (1965). *Handbook of consumer motivations: The psychology of the world of objects.* New York: McGraw-Hill Book Company.

DMA. (2007). *DMA 2007 statistical fact book: The definitive source for direct marketing benchmarks* (29th ed.). New York: Direct Marketing Association.

Fishbein, M., & Aizen, I. (1975). *Belief, attitude, intention, and behavior: An introduction to theory and research.* Reading, MA: Addison-Wesley.

Ford, J. B., Voli, P. K., Honeycutt, E. D., & Casey, S. L. (1998). Gender role portrayals in Japanese advertising: A magazine content analysis. *Journal of Advertising, 27*(1), 113–124.

Frandin, M. P., Martin, E., & Simkin, L. P. (1992). Advertising effectiveness research: A survey of agencies, clients and conflicts. *International Journal of Advertising, 11*, 203–214.

Frazer, C. (1983). Creative strategy: A management perspective. *Journal of Advertising, 12*(4), 36–41.

Frazer, C. F., Sheehan, K. B., & Patti, C. H. (2002). Advertising strategy and effective advertising: Comparing the USA and Australia. *Journal of Marketing Communications, 8*, 149–164.

Gagnard, A., & Morris, J. R. (1988). CLIO commercials from 1975–1985: Analysis of 151 executional variables. *Journalism Quarterly, 65*(4), 859–865.

Haley, R. I., & Baldinger, A. L. (1991). The ARF copy research validity project, *Journal of Advertising Research, 31*(2), 11–32.

Helgesen, T. (1994). Advertising awards and advertising agency performance criteria. *Journal of Advertising Research, 34*(4), 43–53.

Holsti, O. (1969). *Content analysis for the social sciences and the humanities.* Reading, MA: Addison-Wesley.

Huberty, T. (2002). Who's who in ad copytesting. *Quirks Marketing Research Review.* Retrieved March 8, 2005, from http://www. quirks.com/articles/a2002/20020311.aspx?searchID=3431747

Hughes, M. A., & Garrett, D. E. (1990). Intercoder reliability estimation approach in marketing: A generalizability theory framework for quantitative data. *Journal of Marketing Research, 27*(2), 185–195.

Hullett, C. R. (2005). The impact of mood on persuasion: A meta-analysis. *Communication Research, 32*(4), 423–442.

Huhmann, B. A., & Brotherton, T. P. (1997). A content analysis of guilt appeals in popular magazine advertisements. *Journal of Advertising, 26*(2), 35–45.

Hwang, J. S., McMillan, S. J., & Lee, G. (2003). Corporate Web sites as advertising: An analysis of function, audience, and message strategy. *Journal of Interactive Advertising, 3*(2). Retrieved October 8, 2005, from http://www.jiad.org/vol3/no2/mcmillan/

Ji, M. F., & McNeal, J. U. (2001). How Chinese children's commercials differ from those of the United States: A content analysis. *Journal of Advertising, 30*(3), 79–92.

Johar, J. S., & Sirgy, M. J. (1991). Value-expressive versus utilitarian advertising appeals: When and why to use which appeal. *Journal of Advertising, 20*(3), 23–33.

Jones, J. P. (1990). Ad spending: Maintaining market share. *Harvard Business Review, 68*, 38–42.

Kang, N., Kara, A., Laskey, H. A., & Seaton, F. B. (1993). A SAS MACRO for calculating intercoder agreement in content analysis. *Journal of Advertising, 22*(2), 18–28.

Kassarjian, H. H. (1977). Content analysis in consumer research. *Journal of Consumer Research, 4*(2), 8–18.

Katz, H. (2003). *The media handbook.* Mahway, NJ: Lawrence Erlbaum Associates Publishers.

Kelley, S. W., & Turley, L. W. (2004). The effects of content on perceived affect of Super Bowl commercials. *Journal of Sports Management, 18*, 398–420.

Kim, M., & Hunger, J. E. (1993). Attitude–behavior relations: A meta-analysis of attitudinal relevance and topic. *Journal of Communication, 43*(1), 101–142.

Klaassen, A. (2005, November 21). Public won't pay for on-demand content with ads. *Advertising Age, 76*(47), 4.

Kolbe, R. H., & Burnett, M. S. (1991). Content-analysis research: An examination of applications with directives for improving research reliability and objectivity. *Journal of Consumer Research, 18*(3), 243–250.

Korgaonkar, P. K., & Bellinger, D. (1985). Correlates of successful advertising campaigns: The manager's perspective. *Journal of Advertising Research, 25*, 34–39.

Korgaonkar, P. K., Moschis, G. P., & Bellinger, D. (1984). Correlates of successful advertising campaigns. *Journal of Advertising Research, 24*, 47–53.

Kotler, P. (1965). Behavioral models for analyzing buyers. *Journal of Marketing, 22*, 37–45.

Krippendorff, K. (1980). *Content analysis: An introduction to its methodology.* Newbury Park, CA: Sage.

Krugman, H. E. (1965). The impact of television advertising: Learning without involvement. *Public Opinion Quarterly, 29*, 349–356.

Kuhn, T. (1970). *The structure of scientific revolutions* (2nd ed.). Chicago: University of Chicago Press.

Lacy, S., & Riffe, D. (1997). Sampling error and selecting intercoder reliability samples for nominal content categories. *Journalism & Mass Communication Quarterly, 73*(4), 963–973.

Lafayette, J. (2005, October 17). NBC takes $15M off ad shelf; fourth quarter scatter strong: Ratings-challenged Peacock can't cash in. *Television Week.* Retrieved January 20, 2006, from the Lexis-Nexis database.

Lannon, J., & Cooper, P. (1983). Humanistic advertising. *International Journal of Advertising, 2*, 195–213.

Laskey, H., Day, E., & Crask, M. R. (1989). Typologies of main message strategies for television commercials. *Journal of Advertising, 18*(1), 36–41.

Laskey, H., Day, E., & Crask, M. R. (1994). Investigating the impact of executional style on television commercial effectiveness. *Journal of Advertising, 34*(6), 9–16.

Laskey, H., Day, E., & Crask, M. R. (1995). The relationship between advertising message strategy and television commercial effectiveness. *Journal of Advertising Research, 35*(2), 31–39.

Lavidge, R. C., & Steiner, G. A. (1960). A model for predictive measurements of advertising effectiveness. *Journal of Marketing, 25*(4), 59–62.

Leckenby, J. D., & Wedding, N. (1982). *Advertising management: Criteria, analysis and decision making.* Columbus, OH: Grid Publishing Inc.

Little, J. C. (1979). Aggregate advertising models: The state of the art. *Operations Research, 27*(4), 629–665.

Lutz, R. J., MacKenzie, S. B., & Belch, G. E. (1983). Attitude toward the ad as a mediator of advertising effectiveness: Determinants and consequences. In R. P. Bagozzi & A. M. Tybout (Eds.), *Advances in consumer research* (Vol. X, pp. 203–208). Ann Arbor, MI: Association for Consumer Research.

MacInnis, D. J., & Jaworski, B. J. (1989). Information processing from advertisements: Toward an integrative framework. *Journal of Marketing, 53,* 1–23.

MacKenzie, S. B., & Lutz, R. J. (1989). An empirical examination of the structural antecedents of attitude toward the ad in an advertising pretest context. *Journal of Marketing, 53,* 48–65.

Maddox, K. (2006, April 1). Online video ads, new formats grow; Marketers take advantage of emerging technologies to better engage customers. *B to B,* 28.

Maher, J. K., & Childs, N. (2003). A longitudinal content analysis of gender roles in children's television advertisements: A 27 year review. *Journal of Current Issues and Research in Advertising, 25*(1), 71–81.

Mandese, J. (2006, March 21). Magna finds more demand for On-Demand, revises DVR, VOD estimates. *Media Daily News.*

Retrieved April 12, 2006, from http://publications.mediapost.com/ index.cfm?fuseaction=Articles.showAricleHomePage&art_ aid=41229

Mayer, M. (1991). *Whatever happened to Madison Avenue? Advertising in the '90s.* Boston: Little, Brown and Company.

Maynard, M. L., & Taylor, C. R. (1999). Girlish images across cultures: Analyzing Japanese versus U.S. *Seventeen Magazine. Journal of Advertising, 28*(1), 39–48.

McClellan, S. (2006, January 30). Fox and syndication help 5s and 10s gain traction. *Adweek, 47*(5).

McDonald, C. (1993). Point of view: The key is to understand consumer response. *Journal of Advertising Research, 30,* 27–31.

McEwen, W. J., & Leavitt, C. (1976). A way to describe TV commercials. *Journal of Advertising Research, 16*(6), 35–42.

Mehta, A. (2000). Advertising attitudes and advertising effectiveness. *Journal of Advertising Research, 5,* 67–72.

Merriam-Webster Dictionary. (1997). Springfield, MA: Merriam-Webster.

Meyers-Levy, J., & Prashant, M. (1999). Consumers' processing of persuasive advertisements: An integrative framework. *Journal of Marketing, 63,* 45–60.

Moriarty, S. E. (1983). Beyond the hierarchy of effects: A conceptual framework. *Current Issues and Research in Advertising, 4,* 45–55.

Moriarty, S. E. (1996). Effectiveness, objectives, and the EFFIE awards. *Journal of Advertising Research, 36*(4), 54–63.

Mortimer, K. (2002). Integrating advertising theories with conceptual models of service advertising. *Journal of Services Marketing, 16*(5), 460–476.

Mueller, B. (2004). *Dynamics of international advertising: Theoretical and practical perspectives.* New York: Peter Lang.

Myer, J. (2004, July 12). DVR ownership and impact on viewing may be understated [Commentary]. *MediaVillage.* Retrieved January 2, 2005, from http://www.mediavillage. com/jmr/2004/07/12/jmr7-23-04/

Nan, X., & Faber, R. J. (2004). Advertising theory: Reconceptualizing the building blocks. *Marketing Theory, 4*(1–2), 7–30.

Nelson, P. (1970). Information and consumer behavior. *Journal of Political Economy, 78*(2), 729–754.

NMR. (2003). *Channels receivable vs. viewed.* Retrieved April 1, 2006, from http://www.mediainfocenter.org/television/ size/r_vs_viewed.asp

NMR. (2005). *Time spent viewing—Households.* Retrieved April 10, 2006, from http://www.mediainfocenter.org/television/ tv_aud/time_house.asp

Ogilvy, D. (1963). *Confessions of an advertising man.* New York: Ballantine Books.

Okechuky, C., & Wang, C. (1988). The effectiveness of Chinese print ad in North America, *Journal of Advertising Research, 28*(5), 25–34.

Palda, K. S. (1964). On the measurement of advertising effectiveness. *Journal of Advertising Research, 4*(3), 12–16.

Perreault, W. D., & Leigh, L. E. (1989). Reliability of nominal data based on qualitative judgments. *Journal of Marketing Research, 26*(2), 135–148.

Petty, R. E., & Cacioppo, J. T. (1984). The effects of involvement on response to argument quantity and quality: Central and peripheral routes to persuasion. *Journal of Personality and Social Psychology, 46,* 69–81.

Petty, R. E., Cacioppo, J. T., & Schumann, D. (1983). Central and peripheral routes to advertising effectiveness: The moderating role of involvement. *Journal of Consumer Research, 10,* 135–146.

Petty, R. E., Wheeler, S. C., & Bizer, G. Y. (2000). Attitude functions and persuasion: An elaboration likelihood approach to matched versus mismatched messages. In G. Maio & J.Olson (Eds.), *Why we evaluate: Functions of attitudes.* Mahwah, NJ: Lawrence Erlbaum Associates.

Pilotta, J. (2005, August 15). Who cares about engagement? *iMEDIA Connection.* Retrieved March 20, 2006, from http://www.imediaconnection.com/content/6529.asp

Polonsky, M. J., & Waller, D. S. (1995). Does winning advertising awards pay? The Australian experience. *Journal of Advertising Research, 35*(1), 25–35.

Poindexter, P. M., & McCombs, M. E. (2000). *Research in mass communication: A practical guide.* Boston: Bedford/St. Martin's.

Puto, C. P., & Wells, W. D. (1984). Informational and transformational advertising: The differential effects of time. *Advances in Consumer Research, 11,* 638–648.

Ramaprasad, J., & Hasegawa, K. (1992). Creative strategies in American and Japanese TV commercials: A comparison. *Journal of Advertising Research, 32*(1), 59–67.

Ratchford, B. T. (1987). New insights about the FCB grid. *Journal of Advertising Research, 27*, 24–37.

Resnik, A., & Stern, B. L. (1977). An analysis of information content in television advertising. *Journal of Marketing, 41*, 50–53.

Riffe, D., & Freitag, A. (1998). A content analysis of content analyses: Twenty-five years of *Journalism Quarterly. Journalism & Mass Communication Quarterly, 74*(4), 873–882.

Riffe, D., Lacy, S., & Fico, F. (1998). *Analyzing media messages.* Mahwah, NJ: Lawrence Erlbaum Associates.

Rao, R. C. (1986). Estimating continuous time advertising sales models. *Marketing Science, 5*(2), 125–142.

Rogers, R. W. (1983). Cognitive and physiological processes in fear-based attitude change: A revised theory of protection motivation. In J. Cacioppo & R. Petty, (Eds.), *Social psychophysiology. A sourcebook.* New York: Guilford.

Rossiter, J., & Percy, L. (1987). *Advertising and promotions management.* New York: McGraw-Hill.

Rossiter, J. R., Percy, L., & Donovan, R. J. (1991). A better advertising planning grid. *Journal of Advertising Research, 31*(4), 11–21.

Rust, R. (2001). Interrater reliability assessment in content analysis. *Journal of Consumer Psychology, 10*(1), 71–73.

Rust, R. T., & Cooil, B. (1994). Reliability measures for qualitative data: Theory and implications. *Journal of Marketing Research, 31*(2), 1–14.

Schatsky, D. (2006). *The fragmented media future.* Retrieved on April 1, 2006, from http://weblogs.jupiterresearch.com/analysts/schatsky/archives/012845.html

Schreiber, R. J., & Appel, V. (1990). Advertising evaluation using surrogate measures for sales. *Journal of Advertising Research, 30,* 27–31.

Schroer, J. C. (1990). Ad spending: Growing market share. *Harvard Business Review, 68,* 44–48.

Schultz, D. E. (1990). *Strategic advertising campaigns* (3rd ed.). Lincolnwood, IL: NTC Business Books.

Schweitzer, J. C., & Hester, J. B. (1992). The importance of winning advertising award shows. *Southwestern Mass Communication, 7*(1), 55–66.

Scott, W. A. (1955). Reliability of content analysis: The case of nominal scale coding. *Public Opinion Quarterly, 2,* 321–325.

Shimp, T. A. (1974). Unpublished PhD dissertation. University of Maryland.

Spence, P. R., & Lachlan, K. A. (2005). Teaching intercoder reliability: A gentle introduction to content analytic methods for graduate students. *Texas Speech Communication Journal, 30*(1), 71–76.

Spots 'n' Dots. (2006, April 10). *Quarter-billion seen for Nets' Digital Upfront.* Retrieved April 12, 2006, from http://www.spotsndots.com/frameset.asp?f=http://index-zfmw.fimc.net/articlesearch.asp

Steiner, R. L. (1987). Point of view: The paradox of increasing returns in advertising. *Journal of Advertising Research, 27,* 45–53.

Stewart, D. W., & Furse, D. H. (1986). *Effective television advertising: A study of 1,000 commercials.* Lexington, MA: Lexington Books.

Stewart, D. W., & Furse, D. H. (2000). Analysis of the impact of executional factors on advertising performance. *Journal of Advertising Research, 18*(3), 85–89.

Stewart, D. W., & Koslow, S. (1989). Executional factors and advertising effectiveness: A replication. *Journal of Advertising, 18*(3), 21–32.

Stigler, G. (1961). The economics of information. *Journal of Political Economy, 69*(1), 213–225.

Stone, R., & Duffy, M. (1993). Measuring the impact of advertising. *Journal of Advertising Research, 33*(6), RC9–RC12.

Strachan, A. (2005, December 28). Ads now cut 60 minutes of drama to just 42: More television shows littered with longer, badder ads, screen pop-ups in 2005. *Vancouver Sun.* Retrieved from the Lexis-Nexis database.

Taylor, C. R., & Stern, B. B. (1997). Asian-Americans: Television advertising and the "model minority" stereotype. *Journal of Advertising, 26*(2), 47–61.

Taylor, R. E. (1999). A six-segment message strategy wheel. *Journal of Advertising Research, 39*(6), 7–17.

Tellis, G. J. (2004). *Effective advertising: How, when, and why advertising works.* Thousand Oaks, CA: Sage Publications.

Telser, L. G. (1964). Advertising and competition. *Journal of Political Economy, 72*(4), 537–562.

Terazono, E. (2005, September 20). TV fights for its 30 seconds of ad fame. *Financial Times, 1.*

U.S. Census Bureau. (2004). *Number of households with broad-band Internet access.* Retrieved April 1, 2006, from http://www.mediainfocenter.org/interactive/compare/cable_dsl.asp

Vakratsas, D., & Ambler, T. (1999). How advertising works: What do we really know? *Journal of Marketing, 63*, 26–43.

Vaughn, R. (1980). How advertising works: A planning model revisited. *Journal of Advertising Research, 20*(5), 27–34.

Vaughn, R. (1986). How advertising works: A planning model revisited. *Journal of Advertising Research, 26*(1), 57–64.

Veronis Suhler Stevensen. (2004). *Hours per person, per year 2003.* Retrieved March 20, 2006, from http://www.mediainfocenter.org/television/competitive/consumer_media_usage.asp

Walsh, D. (2005, October 21). Heineken calls last orders on television ads after 30 years. *TimesOnline.* Retrieved March 6, 2005, from http://business.timesonline.co.uk/tol/business/industry_sectors/media/article581094.ece

Wells, W. D. (1997). *Measuring advertising effectiveness.* Mahway, NJ: Lawrence Erlbaum Associates.

Wells, W. D., Moriarty, S., & Burnett, J. (2006). *Advertising principles and practice* (7th ed.). Upper Saddle River, NJ: Pearson Prentice Hall.

Wright-Isak, C., Faber, R. J., & Horner, L. R. (1997). Comprehensive measurement of advertising effectiveness: Notes from the marketplace. In W. D. Wells (Ed.), *Measuring advertising effectiveness* (pp. 3–12). Mahway, NJ: Lawrence Erlbaum Associates.

Wyatt, T. J., McCullough, L., & Wolgemuth, W. (1998). A content analysis of television advertising during the 1996 and 1997

NCAA final four basketball tournaments. *Sports Marketing Quarterly, 7*(3), 47–54.

Yssel, Johan C., & Gustafson, R. L. (1998). A strategic analysis of the best television commercial ever produced (worldwide). *Communicatio, 24*(2). Retrieved March 20, 2006, from http://www.unisa.ac.za/default.asp?Cmd=ViewContent&ContentID=7020

Zaichkowsky, J. L. (1985). Measuring the involvement construct. *Journal of Consumer Research, 12*(4), 341–352.

Zajonc, R. B. (1980). Feeling and thinking: Preferences need no inferences. *American Psychologist, 35*, 151–175.

Zajonc, R. B., & Markus, H. (1982). Affective and cognitive factors of preferences. *Journal of Consumer Research, 9*, 121–131.

INDEX

Lightning Source UK Ltd.
Milton Keynes UK
25 February 2010

150554UK00001B/29/P